STITCH New York

20 kooky ways to knit the city and more

Lauren O'Farrell

David and Charles
www.rucraft.co.uk

Contents

Welcome to **Stitch New York**

Starting spreading the news. You're knitting today. You'll make a woolly part of it, New York, New Yooooork.

New York: Nineteen million Gothamites packed into a space where the sounds of the city sing a multi-melodied musical, from dew-damp dawn to dusty dusk and all through the New York night. This is a place where the crosstown traffic relentlessly rumbles past silent puffs of street steam; where the resident red-tailed hawk's city screech is silenced by the Central Park carousel's tinny tune; where the sizzling hot-dog seller's song is drowned out by the crowd-cheered smack of the home run hit heavenwards; and where opulent opera from The Met mingles with the bohemian beat of the Bronx, the cash-register clink of money-munching Manhattan and the distant screams of Coney Island roller-coaster riders.

New York is the city that never stops stitching.

New York's knitters, formed in a yarn-cosied melting pot, are handmade heroes. They'll stitch where they please and what they please, and they're happy to share their small city spaces with more yarn than you ever thought could be packed into a tiny 12th-floor apartment. They have sticks, they have string and – little do non-knitters know – they are taking over the city.

In among the skyscrapers of the concrete jungle's jamboree, New York's many yarn stores thrive on fibre fun; lone knitters stitch on the subway if they can get a seat (though the real stitch sages of the city are well practised at stitching while strap-hanging); Stitch 'n' Bitch groups spring up in coffee-shop corners consuming cocktails and cake; and gutsy graffiti knitters sprinkle their sneaky stitching wherever they wander.

I have always loved New York (what's not to like about a city where you can buy a pretzel as big as your head at 4am?). But when my sticks and string and I landed in the Big Apple on a knitty mission to poke about in its crafty innards for this second city knitting book, I was taken by the handmade and led into a wool-based world of wonder. It was utterly impossible to leave without proclaiming: 'I heart New York knitters'.

Since I'm not a New York native, *Stitch New York* was hatched from the New York we see shining from the silver screen (I stitched and scribbled my way through over 80 New York movies), too many episodes of Seinfeld ('These pretzels are making me thirsty'), five days of running about Manhattan and Brooklyn meeting New York knitters, and from the endless helpful hints of New York know-it-alls on that fabulous world-shrinker we call the internet.

In these pages the Big Apple is a city turned knitty.

PURLING IN PUBLIC

New York knitters are pioneers of the public purl – after all, the first Stitch 'n' Bitch groups sprung up in this knitty city with a handmade hat tip to Ms Debbie Stoller – and are part of the reason I hatched *Stitch London*. As well as being the first book in this city knitting series, *Stitch London* is also the UK's woolly Godzilla of a craft community that has grown up and gone global (there are Stitch Londoners in 52 countries worldwide. Hello NYC Stitch Londoners!) So it seems only right that *Stitch New York* champions getting out in the city and stitching.

Throw a ball of yarn into a New York crowd and you're bound to hit a city knitter (better make it the cheap acrylic stuff. A knitter who throws cashmere is a very wrong knitter indeed). The herds of handmakers who stampede through NYC's annual stitching shows are further proof that New York's knitters are everywhere. And what's more it's a stitched science fact (honest) that knitting in gaggles of giggling fellow fibre flingers gives you a bazillion times more stitching satisfaction than stitching alone.

So grab your woolly work and get out there. New York is rife with knots of knitters with whom you can eat cake, discuss the scandalous shenanigans of Don Draper, eat more cake, clink cocktails, eat more cake, and weep uncontrollably on the shoulders of when you realise you knitted a stitch you were meant to purl 36 rows ago. Dagnabbit! Join an established pack of public purlers, start your own Stitch group (Stitch London welcomes all siblings, as long as you don't borrow our favourite sweater without asking), or just force your existing friends to submit to the knit. Long may the proud tradition of purling in plain sight of all those non-knitters continue to utterly flummox them (and induce that inevitable crafty envy). When you knit in public you inspire others to pick up sticks and string and get their stitch on. And that, my friends, is how world woolly domination begins. MWA HAHAHAHAHAHA!!!

A KNIT NEW YORK STATE OF MIND

Turning New York city knitty isn't about having a wide spectrum of stitching skills. It's all about you, your needles and that squidgy part of you called your brain. Your knitting should be as multi-coloured and multi-flavoured as the city that never stops stitching. There are no rules for what ends up appearing on your knitting needles, and the whole point of these patterns is that you take them and make them your own. Love them, hug them and ask them to be your girl. Sure, if you're a nervous newbie you can stick to the pattern and see how it goes, but knitting is more than just following the handmade herd.

When you take up your sticks and string, you have the potential to conjure up anything with your craft. So if you want your Woolly Woody Allen to end up as a Handmade Howard Stern make it happen (add more hair, darker glasses and fewer visits to the analyst). If you want your Blockbuster Beanie to reflect the fact that you've seen *The Godfather* so many times you're planning on naming your first child (who you hope is a masculine child) Michael Vincent Fredo, then go on and embroider that horse's head on your hat. If you want to turn the Big Bad Burger into a giant knitted lox and a schmear, then do it.

As with all my city knitting books I encourage you to meet my knitting patterns and politely introduce yourself, tell them they look fabulous, get to know them over a cocktail or three, and then unutterably change their identity so they bear only a small family resemblance to the strange stitched creation you met at the start. And don't just stop at changing the yarn. Throw in all manner of handmade madness: buttons, bells, bottle caps, beads, bows, badges, burger sauce… hang on, not burger sauce.

So without further rambling I'd like to welcome you to the woolly world of *Stitch New York*. Where I will now take you by the handmade and lead you on a tour of the knitty city. You'll be starstruck meeting Knit New Yorkers, feel all-American gazing at Little Lady Liberty, and realise if you can make New York there, you can make it anywhere. It's up to you, Noooooo York, Nooooooooooo Yooooooooork!

All Aboard: Exploring Stitch New York

Stitch New York can be explored in any way you like. Steam firmly through from start to finish like a purling power walker, saunter through sprinkling nerd chic and picking pieces that 'speak to you' like a handmaking hipster, or stagger from project to project like a party-hopping stitching socialite.

This section is a friendly helping hand to guide you along the woolly sidewalks of **Stitch New York** patterns, so you can knit without getting in a tangle. The rest is up to you and your trusty needles. Happy travels and have a nice day.

DIFFICULTY RATINGS

How you get around New York and how you get around a knitting pattern share many similarities. You're either a newbie knitter fresh off the plane, all wide-eyed and a little lost; a clued-up stitcher strutting the streets with confidence, a comfy pair of shoes and a fully loaded Metro card; or a stitch sage steering round Columbus Circle and zipping across Brooklyn Bridge like a street-smart New York cabbie.

To help you navigate your way around *Stitch New York's* patterns, here are some handy difficulty levels, with a little New York on the side.

Tourist – Newbie knitters who knit sort of slow and spend a whole lot of time looking up at the tall buildings.

Gothamite – Knitters who know their way around a stitch but sometimes secretly check the map when they're sure nobody is watching.

Yellow Taxicab Driver – Dyed-in-the-wool knitters who have the city map tattooed on their brain and laugh in the face of gridlock.

FIXINGS

'Fixings' means the stuff and things you'll need to make each project: yarn, needles and all those other crafty ingredients that come together to make something woolly and wondrous. See Stitch Essential Fixings for a list of the stuff you won't survive without.

YARN

There is no such thing as 'the right yarn'. The patterns in this book show colour and size of yarn. This gives you an idea of what kind of yarn you need, without loudly insisting you use a specific yarn lest your pattern be cursed. Your yarn is entirely up to you.

For those who must create an exact replica or explode in a cloud of yarn ends, there's a list of some of the yarns used at the back of the book (see Suppliers). However some projects are made from mysterious label-less yarn, which surfaced from the depths of my stash, hungry to be knitted, or were hatched by my giant yarn chicken. But fear not, there'll always be similar yarn for you to use out there.

ABBREVIATIONS

Ahhhh. A little gaggle of knitting abbreviations. So sweet, all tucked into the pattern in neat little rows. Abbreviations are the bits of a knitting pattern that resemble complicated algebraic equations. They're the bits that make non-knitters peering over your shoulder turn slightly green, and need a sit down. They're also the bit that Dumbledore loves the best in the *Harry Potter* books. Roll your eyeballs over this lot and feel free to come back if you forget any.

approx. – approximately
cm – centimetre(s)
DK – double knitting
DPN – double-pointed needle
g – gram(s)
in – inch(es)
inc – increase(s)/increasing
incl – knit through front and back loop of stitch (increase 1 stitch)
k – knit
k2tog – knit 2 stitches together (1 stitch decreased)
m – metre(s)
ml – make one (increase 1 stitch using stitch between 2 stitches)
mm – millimetre(s)

oz – ounces
p – purl
p2tog – purl 2 stitches together (1 stitch decreased)
sl – slip
st(s) – stitch(es)
st st – stocking (stockinette) stitch
tog – together
yd – yards(s)
( ) – repeat instructions in round brackets the number of times indicated

CHANGE UP

These sections shove you gently in the direction of making your knit your own. Quite frankly sticking to the pattern as it's written is for the unadventurous. The whole point of your knitting is that it's yours and nobody else's. So make something that has bits of your brain all over it. Not the actual gooey stuff inside your head, but the ideas that grow in that goo. Your needles are your paintbrush and the yarn is your paint. Change the colour, try out different yarn, chuck in a pair of unexpected googly eyes and see what comes to life.

STITCH ESSENTIAL FIXINGS

Before you embark on your journey through the streets of *Stitch New York*, you will need to arm yourself with some wool-wrangling weapons. Here's a list of stuff you won't survive without.

Knitting needles
Straight needles
Long, straight and pointy in metal, plastic or wood, you're not going to get far without these fellows, so pick ones you like the feel of. You're going to be holding them a lot.

Circular needles
These guys are two needles joined together with a cord. Good for knitting tubes, knitting on transport (they're shorter so are less intrusive when elbow room is tight) or for the wonder of the magic loop (see The Way of the Knit).

Double-pointed needles (DPNs)
They wander in sets or four or five, or even six, and are used for circular knitting. They also seem to fascinate fellow commuters if you bust them out while travelling.

Fixings case

A case in which you stash all the fiddly bits you need when knitting. Pencil cases work well, as do glasses cases, tins, make-up bags or boa constrictors (it can be hard to get the stuff back out of a snake, though).

Darning/tapestry needle

A big fat needle for weaving in ends and sewing up. Get a few, as you will lose some to the hungry Tapestry-needle-eating Monster that stalks us all.

Sewing needle

The fiddly cousins of tapestry needles. These bad boys are ultra-pointy. Be careful where you leave them when not using them. You will find one in your leg at some point in your craft career.

Scissors

Get good, small portable ones that fit in your fixings case. There will be chopping galore.

Tape measure

In the case of most knits, size does matter. A retractable tape measure is the way to go. If it's shaped like Pacman or a giant eyeball even better.

Thread

Always useful for a million things; you can have various colours to hand, but black and white are essential.

Stitch markers

These little rings mark places in your knitting so you don't get lost. So kind. You can buy them or just make them from spare yarn. I use tiny elastic bands for braids.

Crochet hook

This little hook is your 911 emergency aid if you drop a stitch. Use it to pick the stitch back up and fix it. It's also the queen of making long lines of lovely chain stitch. And you can pretend you're a pirate with it.

Small notebook and pen

Scribble down rows, pattern changes or hilarious doodles of your boss being eaten by a sewer alligator while dressed as a Victorian lady.

Project bag

If you can bear to put it down, your WIP (work in progress) is going to need a home when it's not in your hands. If you shove it in your bag and find it's taken a shine to your sunglasses and refuses to be parted from them, well, you'll be sorry. Get a simple drawstring bag, bung it in a plastic bag, or stuff it in a disused sock you stole from a giant.

Stuffing

Forget fancy craft-shop stuffing. Butcher an old pillow or a bargain-shop cushion. Their outsides may be grotty, but their precious innards can be reused.

Beads, buttons and shiny stuff

We're all magpies at heart. Start stashing embellishments where you find them. Snip buttons off holey garments bound for the bin, hoard beads from broken bling and keep your eyes out for bargains.

Eyes

If you only have eyes for the ones you love, you're going to have lots of unfinished WIPs. Bag yourself some safety eyes and seed beads to bring your knits to starey life.

Felt

You can make anything from felt. Anything at all. Honest. If you can't be faffed to knit extra bits, felt works almost as well. Not that I'm suggesting you use felt for everything. But, when in doubt, use felt.

Wire and/or pipe cleaners

Pipe cleaners (chenille stems) and wire give knits their very own skeletons. A bendy knit is a happy knit; just make sure no eyes are poked out by unruly ends. Tuck them in well and bend over tips to round off ends.

NON-ESSENTIAL GUBBINS

Stitch holder

This doohickey is to put stitches on that you're not working for a little while, so you can get on with knitting the others. You can also thread them on a spare bit of yarn (or use a spare needle) if you're a bit skint.

Weights

Tiny character knits sometimes need a little weighing down to keep them upright. You can bag sand, small stones, grain, plastic beads or steel shot (which is what I use) to give your knits a bit of gravity. Just make sure you bag the weight securely, knitting is holey and won't hold it.

Claw clips

Those little crocodile claw clips you use for pinning up long hair are perfect for holding together a seam while you sew it. Get some.

Tweezers

Fiddly crafting, such as stuffing tiny knits or threading beads, is made a thousand times easier with tweezers. Plus you can pluck that unsightly nose hair, too.

Pliers

A pointy pair of craft pliers is good for poking, bending and pulling. Also good for doing crocodile impressions or threatening someone in Mafia style.

Row counter

You click it or roll it each time you complete a row. It remembers it all for you, allowing you to wander off and dream about much more important things, such as how much yarn would fit into the head of the Statue of Liberty if it were your yarn cupboard.

Pins

For stretching out and blocking knits. For voodoo. For cleaning under your nails.

KNITTING TRANSLATIONS

English, on my side of the pond in Blighty and on the other side of the pond in the US isn't quite the same. Autumn is fall, pavements are sidewalks and jam is jelly. We Brits like our words for things to have no connection with their meaning whatsoever; Americans say what they mean. In knitting there are some differences, too. Here's a bit of help if you're lost in translation.

UK term	US term
4ply yarn	sport-weight yarn
cast off	bind off
DK (double knitting) yarn	worsted-weight yarn
double moss stitch	moss stitch
moss stitch	seed stitch
stocking stitch	stockinette stitch
tension	gauge

Needle and hook sizes

Needles, the sticks of your stitching, come in different sizes for different-sized stitches. Just to make things doubly confusing, knitters in the UK and Europe label their sizes differently from the US. Brits and Europeans keep things neatly metric; Americans prefer to throw a nice round number in there. Not all sizes have a direct equivalent in the US, either. You can name them yourself if you like. I'll call that one Englebert.

Knitting needle sizes

Metric	US
2mm	0
2.25mm	1
2.5mm	–
2.75mm	2
3mm	–
3.25mm	3
3.5mm	4
3.75mm	5
4mm	6
4.5mm	7
5mm	8
5.5mm	9
6mm	10
6.5mm	10½
7mm	–
7.5mm	–
8mm	11
9mm	13
10mm	15
12mm	17

Crochet hook sizes

Metric	US
2.25mm	B1
2.5mm	–
2.75mm	C2
3mm	–
3.25mm	D3
3.5mm	E4
3.75mm	F5
4mm	G6
4.5mm	7
5mm	H8
5.5mm	I9
6mm	J10
6.5mm	K10½
8mm	L11
9mm	M/N13
10mm	N/P15
12mm	O16

Yarn weights

UK yarn weights	US yarn weights
2ply	super fine weight
4ply	sport weight
DK	worsted
aran	medium weight
chunky	bulky weight
super chunky	super bulky
Godzilla chunky*	Godzilla bulky*

*Please note: Godzilla-sized yarn is purely fictional. Such a shame.

NYC FILMS THAT STAR KNITTING

Marilyn Monroe, Audrey Hepburn, Julia Roberts and Woody Allen's staple starlet, Diane Keaton, have all bust out their sticks and string on the silver screen. There are a surprising number of NYC films that star a bit of stitching too. Who knew wool could be so Oscar-worthy?

City Lights (1931)
Nothing Sacred (1937)
Shall We Dance (1937)
Mr Skeffington (1944)
Arsenic and Old Lace (1944)
The Glenn Miller Story (1954)
The Seven Year Itch (1955)
The Catered Affair (1956)
Pillow Talk (1959)
Let's Make Love (1959)
Breakfast at Tiffany's (1961)
Up the Down Staircase (1967)
How to Succeed in Business Without Really Trying (1967)
Wait Until Dark (1967)
Rosemary's Baby (1968)
Annie Hall (1977)
Stardust Memories (1980)
Brighton Beach Memoirs (1986)
An American Tale (1986)
Radio Days (1987)
Little Women (1994)
Runaway Bride (1999)
Raising Helen (2004)
Spiderman (2002)
Julie and Julia (2009)
The Friday Night Knitting Club (2013 - apparently)

"Knit New Yorkers

New Yorkers are smart, fast-walking, straight-talking folk. You've got your subway-strap hangers, your sidewalk racers, your cab hailers who know exactly how much to tip. They wait 'on line' not in line, know exactly how long a New York minute is (not very long) and how to pronounce Houston.

They don't **need** to look up. They know their city is all kinds of awesome and they'll gaze at it when they get where they're going, and they're good and ready – possibly over lox and a schmear with a regular cwaffee.

Schlepping your way around the Big Apple you'll get to know some native New Yorkers. So here are some big city hitters to cast on: **Woolly Woody Allen** with added knitted neurosis, delightful **Handmade Holly Golightly** complete with Tiffany's twinkles, and a pair of **Feisty Fibre Firefighters** in case of emergencies, New York's Bravest at their yarny best. Fuhgeddaboudit!

Now, will youze get outta the way? I'm walkin' here!

Woody missed New York's radio days...

I'm just CRAZY about Tiffany's!

WOOLLY WOODY ALLEN

'New York was his town, and it always would be…' Woody Allen is the undisputed bespectacled, neurotic, awkward king of New York. His city of skyscrapers, endless shrink visits, escaped lobsters, Central Park rainstorms, overbearing mothers and Hudson River-side romantic strolls are the stuff true city stories are made of. Knit Woolly Woody Allen and you can live with a New York icon without having to give up too much room in your apartment. Just don't ask him to explain women to you. You'll be there a loooooooooong time.

FIXINGS

Needles
Set of four 3.25mm (US size 3) double-pointed needles or circular needle for magic loop (see The Way of the Knit)

Yarn
8g (⅓oz) light pink DK (worsted) yarn for skin
5g (⅙oz) red DK (worsted) yarn for shirt
5g (⅙oz) brown DK (worsted) yarn for trousers
Small amount of brown mohair yarn for hair

Other stuff
Stitch marker
Stuffing
Scissors
Tapestry needle
Black or brown felt for feet
Brown embroidery thread for shirt and shoes
White embroidery thread for buttons
Around 15cm (6in) black wire/pipe cleaner for glasses (or wrap plain wire in black tape)
Seed beads for eyes
Sewing needle and black thread
Neurosis (optional)

Difficulty rating: Gothamite
Size: Approx. 12cm (4¾in) tall
Gauge: Not important

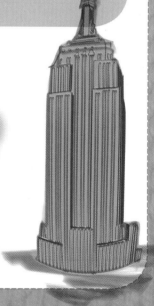

PATTERN

Head, body and legs

Cast on 3 sts in light pink yarn.
Row 1 Incl three times (6 sts).
Divide sts between three needles, place marker at start of round and join to knit in the round.
Round 2 K around.
Round 3 Incl around (12 sts).
Round 4 K around.
Round 5 (K, incl) around (18 sts).
Round 6 K around.
Round 7 (K2, incl) around (24 sts).
Round 8 K around.
Round 9 (K3, incl) around (30 sts).
Round 10 K around.
Round 11 (K4, incl) around (36 sts).
Round 12 K around.
Round 13 K around.
Round 14 (K, k2tog) around (24 sts).
Round 15 K around.
Round 16 (K2, k2tog) around (18 sts).
Round 17 K around.
Round 18 (K, k2tog) around (12 sts).
Round 19 K around.
Round 20 K around.
Stuff head.

> Don't stuff a Knit New Yorker's head too much or it'll start to look alien and end up being cast in **X-Files** remakes.

Change to red yarn for shirt.
Rounds 21–23 K around.
Round 24 (K, incl) around (18 sts).
Rounds 25–27 K around.
Change to brown yarn for trousers.
Rounds 28–34 K around.

Cast off (bind off) tightly leaving 15cm (6in) tail.
Stuff body leaving legs unstuffed.
Use tail of yarn to sew back and front of trousers together up the centre, to form two legs that are joined in the middle. Lightly stuff both legs.

> Change body shape and height for your Knit New Yorkers by changing how much stuffing you use and by piling on more or less hair. No harsh workouts for these little fellas.

Arms (make 2)

Cast on 3 sts in red yarn.
Push sts to other end of needle.
Knit 7 rows as I-cord.
Cut yarn with long tail, thread through sts and pull tight.
Darn in tail at cast-on end of arm.
Using light pink yarn, sew through cast-on end eight times to make hand.

FINISHING

Use tail from arms to sew arms to body at shoulder height.
Embroider ears by using light pink yarn to sew into one stitch on each side of head eight times.
Embroider nose by using light pink yarn to sew into one stitch in the middle of the face six times.
Embroider hair by using brown mohair yarn to sew a few stripes of hair just above the ears from the front to the back of the head. Do the same on the middle of the head (leaving two areas either side for the receding hairline (sorry Woody).
Cut two ovals from brown felt to make feet.
Sew ovals onto legs using brown embroidery thread.
Use the same thread to make a shoelace bow on the front of each shoe at the base of each foot.

> Woody Allen film fact: knitting features in **Annie Hall**, **Radio Days** and **Stardust Memories**. Cool, no?

Use brown embroidery thread (about three strands thick) to sew vertical and horizontal stripes onto shirt.

Use white embroidery thread to make three buttons on shirt front.

Bend a 15cm (6in) wire/pipe cleaner to make square glasses (you can bend it around the square end of a chopstick to get a good corner). If pipe cleaner is too fluffy, wrap in electrical tape to give it that plastic look.

Sew on seed beads for eyes, using a sewing needle and black thread.

Pop on specs so he can see.

Book appointment with analyst.

Always sew on a Knit New Yorker's eyes last of all. You don't want them peering at you while you're jabbing needles into their heads - trust me.

CHANGE UP

Once you get the hang of knitting a Knit New Yorker you have the potential to create anyone at all. Change the threads, bust out a whole new hairdo, or orange them up with fake tan. The purly people of the city that never sleeps are yours to create (whether they're fictional or flesh and blood). Fling on a fedora and whip up a woolly horse's head to create a crafty Don Corleone, take it all off and slap on a hat to make the infamous knitty Naked Cowboy, or add curly locks and a pair of hideously expensive Manolos for a stitched Sarah Jessica Parker.

HANDMADE HOLLY GOLIGHTLY

'The only thing that does any good is to jump in a cab and go to Tiffany's. Calms me down right away. The quietness and the proud look of it; nothing very bad could happen to you there.'

Miss Holly Golightly is New York from the top of her French twist to the tips of her alligator shoes. New York sways to the melodic strum of her fire-escape guitar playing, happily hands over bills for her $50 bathroom visits, and rattles its ice cubes in countless cocktail glasses at her all-night parties. What a gal she is.

Handmade Holly will munch pastry and sip coffee with you while gazing into the windows at Tiffany & Co in the early hours; she'll get shushed book hunting with you in the public library; she'll ring every doorbell in the building for you if you forget your key; and she'll visit you at Sing Sing should you find yourself on the wrong side of the law. Since Holly is a knitter too, she might even settle down to knit with you, though you might end up with a ranch house rather than the jumper you set out to make.

FIXINGS

Needles
Set of four 3.25mm (US size 3) double-pointed needles or circular needle for magic loop (see The Way of the Knit)

Yarn
8g (⅓oz) light pink DK (worsted) yarn for skin
8g (⅓oz) black DK (worsted) yarn for dress
5g (⅙oz) dark brown DK (worsted) yarn for hair
A teeny, tiny bit of orange yarn for the tip of Holly's lit cigarette

Other stuff
Stitch marker
Stuffing
Scissors
Tapestry needle
Black felt for feet
Black embroidery thread to sew feet
Brown embroidery thread to help position hair
1 cotton bud for cigarette and holder
Black marker pen
Sewing needle and black thread
Stick-on diamonds: 1 large (about 1cm (½in) across), 1 medium sized and about 20 small for necklace and earrings
Glue
Seed beads for eyes
Melody to *Moon River* to hum dreamily while you're knitting (optional)

Difficulty rating: Gothamite
Size: 12cm (4¾in) tall
Gauge: Not important

PATTERN

Head, body and legs

Cast on 3 sts in light pink yarn.
Row 1 Inc1 three times (6 sts).
Divide sts between three needles, place marker at start of round and join to knit in the round.
Round 2 K around.
Round 3 Inc1 around (12 sts).
Round 4 K around.
Round 5 (K, inc1) around (18 sts).
Round 6 K around.
Round 7 (K2, inc1) around (24 sts).
Round 8 K around.
Round 9 (K3, inc1) around (30 sts).
Round 10 K around.
Round 11 (K4, inc1) around (36 sts).
Round 12 K around.
Round 13 K around.
Round 14 (K, k2tog) around (24 sts).
Round 15 K around.
Round 16 (K2, k2tog) around (18 sts).
Round 17 K around.
Round 18 (K, k2tog) around (12 sts).
Round 19 K around.
Round 20 K around.
Stuff head.

Try not to be a 'thumping bore'. Holly will not approve.

Round 21 K around.
Round 22 K around.

Change to black yarn.
Round 23 K around.
Round 24 (K, inc1) around (18 sts).
Rounds 25–34 K around.
Cast off (bind off).
Stuff body and legs.

Arms (make 2)

Cast on 3 sts in pink yarn.
Push sts to other end of needle.
Knit 3 rows as I-cord (see The Way of the Knit).
Change to black yarn.
Knit 4 rows as I-cord.
Cut yarn with long tail, thread through sts and pull tight.
Darn in all yarn ends except cast-on tail (which you will use to sew arm to body).

FINISHING

Use tail from arms to sew arms to body at shoulder height.
Embroider ears by using light pink yarn to sew into one stitch on each side of head eight times.
Embroider nose by using light pink yarn to sew into one stitch in the middle of the face six times.
Cut a felt circle with two smaller circles sticking out for feet.
Sew circle onto base of body using black embroidery thread.
Use black yarn doubled over to embroider straps and back of dress.

Make hair

Holly's updo is easy-peasy to create in yarn. Using dark brown yarn, make a small ball of yarn about 1cm (½in) in size. Cut the yarn, tuck the end in (you can use a tapestry needle) and put the ball to one side.
Make a rope by making six 20cm (8in) loops of yarn and holding them together. Using brown embroidery thread, sew the end of the rope with the tails to the front right of the head

Watch out for those 'mean reds'. That means keeping Handmade Holly well away from that nasty scarlet eyelash yarn you bought on a crazy whim.

(it doesn't matter how it looks as you're going to cover it up. Just make sure it's secure). Now coil the hair around the back of Holly's head sewing in place as you go. Coil it round and round until you reach the middle with a 2–3cm (1–1½in) of rope to spare. Sew the middle into place and then twist the remaining rope into a tighter rope to form the 'twist' part of the hair. Sew it carefully onto the back of the head. Sew the ball of yarn on top of the head et voila! A French twist up-do!

Make cigarette holder

Cut the ends off the cotton bud. Colour two-thirds of the tube with black marker pen. Poke a piece of orange yarn into the end of the tube to make the lit end of the cigarette. Sew holder onto Holly's hand using black thread.

If you take your handmade Holly to a party, keep an eye on her. If you don't watch it she'll end up engaged to someone who simply isn't good enough for her. The cad! You don't want her tiny knitted heart unravelling, do you?

Make Holly sparkle

Use glue to stick the large 'diamond' to the front of Holly's hair. Make sure only the top half is showing to form the tiara. If you have trouble with this try cutting it in half (this won't work if it's a real diamond). Glue the medium-sized 'diamond' to the middle of the dress front. Glue smaller stones around the top of the dress to make a necklace. Glue one 'diamond' to each ear.

Sew on seed beads for eyes, using a sewing needle and black thread. Mix Holly a Sidecar in a tall glass and prepare for a night on the town. And don't forget that $50 for the bathroom.

CHANGE UP

The Holly on the silver screen has all manner of outfits and so, too, could yours. Knit her in a striking orange coat for an afternoon of shoplifting, drape her in a white chemise and satin sleep mask or make her a snazzy sequin-bejewelled dress. To be honest she'd look gorgeous wearing a trash bag. Sigh.

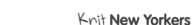

FIESTY FIBRE FIREFIGHTERS

New York's Bravest, the firefighters of the New York Fire Dept are an amazing bunch. Besides fighting flames they wrangle search and rescue, are first on the scene in an emergency, and are pretty handy at rescuing cats from trees. Bad kitty! NYFD's 11,500 uniformed firefighters are a close-knit family of lifesavers and their city is overwhelmingly proud of each and every one of them. What better way to give a woolly salute than to create your very own Feisty Fibre Firefighters.

FIXINGS

Needles
Set of four 3.25mm (US size 3) double-pointed needles or circular needle for magic loop (see The Way of the Knit)

Yarn
8g (⅓oz) skin colour DK (worsted) yarn for skin
8g (⅓oz) black DK (worsted) yarn for uniform and hat
Small amount of bright yellow DK (worsted) yarn for reflective bands
Small amount of DK (worsted) yarn in a colour of your choice for hair

Other stuff
Stitch marker
Stuffing
Scissors
Tapestry needle
Black felt for feet, hat brim and badge
Black embroidery thread for sewing feet and hat
White embroidery thread for helmet number
Seed beads for eyes
Sewing needle and black thread
Fearlessness in spade loads (not optional)

Difficulty rating: Gothamite
Size: Approx. 12cm (4¾in) tall
Gauge: Not important

PATTERN

Head, body and legs

Cast on 3 sts in skin colour yarn.
Row 1 Inc1 three times (6 sts).
Divide sts between three needles,
place marker at start of round and
join to knit in the round.
Round 2 K around.
Round 3 Inc1 around (12 sts).
Round 4 K around.
Round 5 (K, inc1) around (18 sts).
Round 6 K around.
Round 7 (K2, inc1) around (24 sts).
Round 8 K around.
Round 9 (K3, inc1) around (30 sts).
Round 10 K around.
Round 11 (K4, inc1) around (36 sts).
Round 12 K around.
Round 13 K around.
Round 14 (K, k2tog) around (24 sts).
Round 15 K around.
Round 16 (K2, k2tog) around (18 sts).
Round 17 K around.
Round 18 (K, k2tog) around (12 sts).
Round 19 K around.
Round 20 K around.
Stuff head.

Change to black yarn.
Rounds 21–24 K around.
Round 25 (K, inc1) around (18 sts).
Rounds 26–35 K around.
Cast off (bind off).

Arms (make 2)

Cast on 3 sts in black yarn.
Push sts to other end of needle.
Knit 7 rows as I-cord (see The Way
of the Knit).
Cut yarn with long tail, thread through
sts and pull tight.
Darn in tail at cast-on end of arm.

Using skin-coloured yarn, sew through
cast-on end eight times to make hand.

Hat

Cast on 3 sts in black yarn.
Row 1 Inc1 three times (6sts).
Divide sts between three needles, place
marker at start of round and join to
knit in the round.
Round 2 K around.
Round 3 Inc1 around (12 sts).
Round 4 Inc1 around (24 sts).
Round 5 (K3, inc1) around (30 sts).
Round 6 (K4, inc1) around (36 sts)
Rounds 7–11 K around.
Round 12 (K4, k2tog) around (30 sts).
Cast off (bind off) tightly leaving 15cm
(6in) tail.
Stuff body leaving legs unstuffed.
Use tail of yarn to sew back and front
of trousers together up the centre, to
form two legs that are joined in the
middle. Lightly stuff both legs.

FINISHING

Use tail from arms to sew arms to
body at shoulder height.
Embroider ears by using skin colour
yarn to sew into one stitch on each
side of head eight times.
Embroider nose by using skin colour
yarn to sew into one stitch in the
middle of the face six times.
Add hair – there are loads of different
ways to do this, so go wild. (The
blonde male firefighter's hair is made
from short loops sewn to make a
side parting. The dark-haired female
firefighter has long silky yarn sewn in
the middle for a centre parting and tied
up at the back).

Cut two felt ovals from black felt to make feet.

Sew ovals onto feet using black embroidery thread.

Use the same thread to make a bootlace bow on the front of each shoe at the base of each foot.

Use bright yellow yarn to sew stripes around body, legs and arms of fire fighters.

Sew black yarn around neck to make collar; down middle of jacket to make jacket front; and around waist to separate trousers from jacket.

Make hat

Place the bowl of the hat on a piece of black felt and cut a circle that is 1cm (½in) bigger to make the brim of the hat.

Cut an X in the middle of the circle stopping 1cm (½in) short of the edge.

Fold each triangle cut from the X into the side of the bowl of the hat to attach brim to hat.

Sew the rest of the circle around the brim to make brim flush against bowl of hat.

Cut a shield shape approx. 12mm (½in) wide in black felt.

With 'point' of shield shape at the top, embroider number of your choice and the initials NYFD using white embroidery thread.

Stick or sew badge onto front of hat, using black embroidery thread.

Sew on seed beads for eyes, using a sewing needle and black thread.

Pop hat on head.

Scan the area for danger so your firefighter can leap in to avert it.

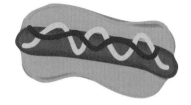

Put your tiny fire helmet on your cat when he's least expecting it. He'll look suddenly hilarious and oddly attractive.

CHANGE UP

You can adapt your Feisty Fibre Firefighter to make all kinds of NYC heroes. From all-knowing cabbies, to all-night pancake flippers, to all-seeing cops. None of them will be quite as handsomely heroic as the ladies and gents from the NYFD though. They're ever so dreamy.

Mini Metropolis

New York is a city of skyscrapers. In between them, the citizens scurry and the traffic trundles along 6,000 miles of streets. Flying in to JFK, floating in across the Atlantic or rolling in across Brooklyn Bridge the sight of the skyline slaps you in the face in silver-screen style.

A forest of over 550 skyscrapers casts some of the world's longest shadows and has impressively speedy elevators (aaaaaiiiiiieeeee!). There are over 800 miles of subway in New York's rumbling belly and 843 acres of Central Park to get lost in (didn't you just pass that pretzel stand?).

To help you find your bearings, here are a few knitty NYC landmarks by which to navigate and a set of woolly wheels to get you where you need to go. **Little Lady Liberty** gives a woolly wave with her fibre-based flaming torch; a small but stately **Squishy Empire State** nods wisely from above; and a **Small Yellow Taxi** waits impatiently to zoom you through the gritty grid of city streets. Grab some cab fare, your metro card and a pair of good walking shoes and get outta here!

Give me your knits, your purls, your handmade makings...

Mom? Is that you?

SMALL YELLOW TAXI

TAXI! New York's 13,000 cabs are the bright yellow lifeblood of the city, rushing through the tarmac traffic to take you where you want to go with a honk, a swerve and another honk. Their drivers may be from all over the world, but they are the city's sages. They know their uptown from their downtown, and their BQE from their GWB. And they'll tell you all about it if you climb in – whether you want to hear it or not.

This Small Yellow Taxi is raring for you to take a ride. She's a knitted checkered cab from the days of taxis gone by. Stitch her together, stick on her wheels and watch her go. This little knit actually rolls! Just keep an eye on that meter. She tends to overcharge if you don't pay attention. Is this really the shortest route to the Met? And don't forget to tip!

Difficulty: Yellow Taxicab Driver
Size: 11 x 6cm (4⅓ x 2⅓in)
Gauge: 22 sts and 30 rows = 10cm (4in) in st st

FIXINGS

Needles
Pair of 4mm (US size 6) straight needles

Yarn
20g (⅔oz) bright yellow DK (worsted) yarn for the main colour
Small amount of light blue DK (worsted) yarn for the windows
Small amount of black and white DK (worsted) yarn for the checker pattern

Other stuff
Scraps of yarn in four different colours for markers
Scissors
2 x stitch holders (or spare needles)
Scraps of another colour yarn to mark folds
Tapestry needle
6 x 6cm (2⅓ x 2⅓in) piece of foam filling
11 x 6cm (4⅓ x 2⅓in) piece of foam filling (I cut up a small sponge)
Around 2.5cm (1in) square of black felt for sign
White embroidery thread
Black embroidery thread
Glue gun
Small amount of silver thread for metal
2 x silver sequins for headlights
2 x red sequins for brake lights
13cm (5in) long wooden skewer
Tape measure
4 x round black buttons
1 x plastic drinking straw (average sized – no skinny straws; normal fast food straws are best)

PATTERN NOTES

The Small Yellow Taxi is knit in two pieces: sides and bottom are one piece; front, back and top the other. They are then sewn together to make the 3D shape. It's easier than it sounds. Honest.

PATTERN

Sides and bottom
Window 1
Cast on 12 sts in light blue yarn, using cable cast-on (see The Way of the Knit).
Row 1 K across. Mark middle of row with scrap yarn (this is Marker 1).
Row 2 P across.
Row 3 K10, inc1, k (13 sts).
Row 4 P across.
Row 5 K11, inc1, k (14 sts).
Row 6 P across.
Cut yarn with 10cm (4in) tail and place on holder.

Side 1
Cast on 5 sts in bright yellow yarn using cable cast-on. Cut yarn with a 10cm (4in) tail.
Place blue sts back on the needle, next to the new yellow sts with the knit side facing.
On the same needle cast on 6 sts in bright yellow.
Row 7 K across all sts in bright yellow (25 sts).
Row 8 P across.
Row 9 K across.
Row 10 K across.
Row 11 Change to white yarn and black yarn. K across, alternating sts in white then black to end of row, starting with white.
Row 12 P across, alternating sts in black and white to end, starting with black.
Row 13 Change to yellow. K across.
Row 14 P across.
Row 15 K across.

Bottom
Change to black yarn.
Rows 16–24 Work in st st starting with purl row.
Row 25 Mark start of row with scrap yarn (this is Marker 2). K across.
Row 26 Mark start of row with scrap yarn (this is Marker 3). P across.
Rows 27–34 Work in st st starting with a knit row.

Side 2
Change to bright yellow yarn.
Row 35 K across.
Row 36 P across.

Row 37 K across.
Row 38 Change to white yarn and black yarn. P across, alternating sts in black then white to end of row, starting with black.
Row 39 K across, alternating sts in white and black to end, starting with white.
Row 40 P across.
Row 41 P across.
Row 42 K across.
Row 43 P across.

Window 2
Row 44 Cast off (bind off) four sts knitwise. Cut yarn, leaving 10cm (4in) tail. Change to light blue yarn. Cast off (bind off) one st. K13. Change to yellow yarn. Cast off (bind off) 6 sts knitwise. Cut yarn leaving 10cm (4in) tail.
Row 45 Change to light blue yarn. K11, k2tog, k (13 sts).
Row 46 P across.
Row 47 K10, k2tog, k (12 sts).
Row 48 P across.
Row 49 K across.
Cast off (bind off) all sts. Cut yarn leaving 10cm (4in) tail. Mark middle of row with scrap yarn (this is Marker 4).

Front, roof and back
Front end
Cast on 14 sts in bright yellow yarn.
Row 1 K across. Mark middle of row with same colour scrap yarn as Marker 3.
Rows 2–5 Work in st st starting with purl row.
Row 6 P across. Mark each end with the scrap yarn for showing where to fold the front section to make the bonnet (hood).
Row 7 K across.
Row 8 P across.
Row 9 K across.
Rows 10–13 Work in st st starting with purl row.

Windshield
Row 14 Change to light blue yarn. P across.
Row 15 K across.
Row 16 P across.
Row 17 K across.
Row 18 P across.
Row 19 K across.

Roof
Row 20 Change to bright yellow yarn. P across.
Rows 21–34 Work in st st starting with a knit row.
Row 35 K across.
Row 36 P across.
Row 37 Mark start of row with Marker 1 yarn. K across.
Row 38 Mark start of row with Marker 4 yarn. P across.

Rows 39–40 Work in st st starting with a knit row.

Rear window

Rows 41–44 Change to light blue yarn. Work in st st starting with a knit row.
Row 45 P across. Mark each end with the scrap yarn for showing where to fold the end section to make the boot (trunk).
Rows 46–52 Work in st st starting with purl row.
Cast off (bind off) all sts.
Mark middle of cast-off (bound-off) row with Marker 2 yarn.

FINISHING

Assembling the taxi

Using bright yellow yarn, sew both knit pieces together by matching up the 1, 3 and 4 markers on each piece (for example, Marker 1 on Side and Bottom to Marker 1 on Front, Roof and Back).

Leave the Marker 2 end open for stuffing.
Use the unnumbered markers to show you where to make folds for the hood and trunk, and match up the blue window pieces.
Push smaller foam block into top of taxi to shape roof and windows.
Push larger foam block into taxi to shape sides, front and back. You may have to push and pull it around so the corners are correctly positioned.
Sew up the last seam (Marker 2 on Side and Bottom to Marker 2 on Front, Roof and Back).

Final touches

Using bright yellow yarn, embroider down the sides of the front and back windows. Embroider dividing lines on both side windows (see picture).
Using white thread, embroider 'TAXI' on the black felt square. Fold felt in half and use black thread to sew the edges

to close (or glue in place). Sew on to top of taxi at front of roof.
Use silver thread to embroider front grille and door handles.
Sew or stick on two silver sequins for headlights.
Sew or stick on two red sequins for brake lights.
Cut skewer into two 6.5cm (2½in) lengths. Using a glue gun, glue a button to one end of each skewer.
Make sure they are dead centre – this

is very important for allowing the wheels to roll. Leave to dry.

Cut straw into two 6cm (2⅓in) lengths. Push each length into knitting at the bottom of the car between the fabric and the sponge where the wheels will go. They should just fit through the stitches and poke out slightly at each end. Hold them in place with a blob of glue if necessary. Just don't get any glue in the ends of the straw.

When dry push one buttoned skewer through the front straw. Dot glue into the centre of another button and hold it onto the other end of the skewer until it dries. Again keep it dead centre. Repeat with the second buttoned skewer and last button.

Once the glue has dried (please let it dry. Sticky glue will get caught up and

you'll end up with a car with no go. So sad), give your taxi a push to see how she goes. If she's a little wobbly on her wheels try taking them off, removing the glue (it should peel off) and redoing it until you get it right. You see what I meant about dead centre now.

Woo hoo! Your Small Yellow Taxi can now motor. Look out for a stranded tourist for your first fare.

Zoom your Small Yellow Taxi past your cat for 'giant radioactive cat attacks city' perspective.

CHANGE UP

The four-wheeled woolly possibilities are endless. Use the Small Yellow Taxi pattern to turn her into a siren-wailing cop car, a classic Cadillac or a showy stretch limo. HOOOOONK! HOOOOOONK!!!

SQUISHY EMPIRE STATE

FIXINGS

Needles
Pair of 4mm (US size 6) straight needles
Pair of 4mm (US size 6) double-pointed needles or circular needle for I-cord (see The Way of the Knit)

Yarn
35g (1¼oz) grey DK (worsted) yarn
Small amount of silver crochet yarn for windows

Other stuff
Scissors
Tapestry needle
6cm (2⅓in) plastic tube for top (I used an old pen lid)
5cm (2in) foam cube for top
7 × 7 × 22cm (2¾ × 2¾ × 8⅔in) firm foam block
Small bag of something heavy, not more than 4cm (1½in) wide (to help tower stand more easily). You can use rice, sand, dark matter or store-bought stuff. I used steel shot.
7cm (2¾in) square of cardboard for base

In 1931 the Empire State Building was the tallest skyscraper in the whole world. What a guy. He's also rubbed shoulders with some of the greats. King Kong swatted angrily at aeroplanes from its tower, Cary Grant hung about its observation deck heedless of the plight of his lady love in the streets far below and *Independence Day* aliens blew it to smithereens.

Stitching a life-sized skyscraper might be ambitious but this Squishy Empire State is more manageable. He's woolly, but he likes to think he retains the stature of his concrete-and-steel big bro. Just don't call him small. A sulky skyscraper is a sad thing.

Difficulty rating: Tourist
Size: 38cm (15in) tall
Gauge: 22 sts and 25 rows = 10cm (4in) in st st

PATTERN

Tower

Cast on 51 sts in grey yarn, using cable cast-on (see The Way of the Knit).

Row 1 K12, p, k12, p, k4, p4, k4, p, k12.
Row 2 P12, k, p4, k4, p4, k, p12, k, p12.
Rows 3–60 Repeat rows 1 and 2.
Row 61 (K2tog twice, k4, k2tog twice, p) three times, (k2tog, k2, k2tog) twice (35 sts).
Row 62 P8, k, p8, k, p8, k, p8.
Row 63 (K2tog, k4, k2tog, p) three times, k2tog, k4, k2tog (27 sts).
Row 64 P6, k, p6, k, p6, k, p6.
Row 65 K6, p, k6, p, k6, p, k6.
Row 66 Repeat row 64.
Row 67 (K2tog, k2, k2tog, p) three times, k2tog, k2, k2tog (19 sts).
Row 68 (P2tog twice, k) three times, p2tog twice (11 sts).
Row 69 K2tog, k, k2tog, k, k2tog, k, k2tog (7 sts).
Rows 70–80 Work in st st starting with a purl row.
Row 81 K2tog twice, k, k2tog (4 sts).
Change to DPNs or circular needle.
Rows 82–85 Knit as I-cord.
Cut yarn and thread through remaining sts. Pull tight, knot and darn in end.

The real Empire State Building is struck by lightning 100 times a year. Yours is much smaller so expect only a handful of lightning strikes.

Deter giant apes from climbing your Squishy Empire State by not allowing disarmingly beautiful wannabe actresses from hanging about it. And don't eat bananas around it either.

Base

Cast on 15 sts in grey yarn, using cable cast-on.
Knit 20 rows.
Cast off (bind off).

FINISHING

Sew together long seams of tower to make a tube.
Push plastic tube into top of tower to make spike.

Place small foam cube into top of tower.

Place tall foam block inside tower, leaving room at the bottom to insert steel shot, or similar.

Insert steel shot (you may have to make a hole in the foam for it to squash into).

Place 7cm (2¾in) cardboard square in bottom of tower before stitching the knit base in place.

Embroider silver windows on sides.

Keep on embroidering windows.

Blimey. There really are a lot of windows.

Beat your chest in a King Kong style. You've created one heck of a giant building. Have a banana to celebrate.

Dropping a penny from the top of your Squishy Empire State could result in passersby looking around to see if they've dropped change... and not much else really.

CHANGE UP

The Squishy Empire State could be shuffled about to be any skyscraper in the world: decrease early on your way up for London's pointy Shard, double it up for Kuala Lumpur's petrifyingly high Petronas Towers or throw is some ridges for Taiwan's fantabulous Taipei 101.

LITTLE LADY LIBERTY

Zut alors! There's a giant French lady standing on Liberty Island, waving a flaming torch and dressed in only a toga. No one seems even slightly worried?! New Yorkers turn a blind eye to the craziest things. The lovely Lady Liberty is a whopping 46m tall in her size 879 sandals, and she's here to dispense humongous green liberty, enlightenment and independence, dammit. Little Lady Liberty is just as sassy despite her size, and fancies a night on the town, *Ghostbusters 2* style. Knit her up and take her partying. She'll have a Big Appletini on the rocks, shaken and not stirred.

FIXINGS

Needles
Set of four 4mm (US size 6) double-pointed needles or circular needle for magic loop (see The Way of the Knit)
Pair of four 4mm (US size 6) straight needles

Yarn
25g (⅞oz) copper green DK (worsted) yarn
Small amount of gold yarn for torch

Other stuff
Stitch marker
Scissors
Stuffing
1 × 30cm (12in) pipe cleaner for arms
Scrap of yarn in a contrasting colour
Small bag of something heavy not more than 4cm (1½in) wide (to help Liberty stand more easily). You can use rice, sand, dark matter or store-bought stuff. I used steel shot. Optional, but adds anti-hunting bonus.
Small amount of cardboard for bottom
Tapestry needle
Beads for eyes
Sewing needle and black thread
3 × 3.5cm (1¼ × 1½in) card for tablet
Black embroidery thread for tablet

Difficulty rating: Yellow Taxicab Driver
Size: Approx. 18cm (7in) tall
Gauge: Not important

PATTERN

Head, body and legs

Using DPNs, cast on 3 sts in copper green yarn.

Row 1 Inc1 three times (6 sts).

Divide sts between three DPNs, place marker at start of round and join to knit in the round.

Round 2 and all even rounds to Round 14 K around.

Round 3 Inc1 around (12 sts).

Round 5 (K, inc1) around (18 sts).

Round 7 (K2, inc1) around (24 sts).

Round 9 (K3, inc1) around (30 sts).

Round 11 (K4, inc1) around (36 sts).

Round 13 (K5, inc1) around (42 sts).

Round 15 and all odd rounds to Round 23 K around.

Round 16 (K5, k2tog) around (36 sts).

Round 18 (K, k2tog) around (24 sts).

Round 20 (K2, k2tog) around (18 sts).

Round 22 (K, k2tog) around (12 sts).

Rounds 24–26 K around.

Stuff head.

Round 27 (K, inc1) around (18 sts).

Round 28 K around.

Round 29 (K2, inc1) around (24 sts).

Rounds 30–80 K around.

Cast off (bind off).

Bottom

Using straight needles, cast on 3 sts.

Row 1 Inc1, k inc1, (5 sts).

Row 2 K across.

Row 3 K, inc1, k, inc1, (7 sts).

Row 4 K across.

Row 5 K, inc1, k3, inc1, k (9 sts).

Row 6 K across.

Row 7 K, inc1, k5, inc1, k (11 sts).

Rows 8–10 K across.

Row 11 K, k2tog, k5, k2tog, k (9 sts).

Row 12 and all even rows to Row 16 K across.

Row 13 K, k2tog, k3, k2tog, k (7 sts).

Row 15 K, k2tog, k, k2tog, k, (5 sts).

Row 17 K2tog, k, k2tog (3 sts).

Cast off (bind off).

Arms (make 2)

Using straight needles, cast on 5 sts.

Knit 15 rows as I-cord.

Thread yarn through sts and tie off. Cut pipe cleaner in half and bend each half in two. Push pipe cleaner into arm from cast-on end leaving 2cm (¾in) sticking out of cast-on end.

Robe: right shoulder

Using straight needles, cast on 8 sts using cable cast-on (see The Way of the Knit).

Rows 1–8 Work in st st starting with knit row.

Row 9 K, k2tog twice, k3 (6 sts).

Row 10 P across.

Row 11 K, k2tog, k3 (5 sts).

Row 12 P across.

Row 13 K across.

Row 14 P across.

Row 15 K, inc1, k3 (6 sts).

Row 16 P across.

Row 17 K, inc1 twice, K3 (8 sts).

Rows 18–25 Work in st st starting with purl row.

Cast off (bind off).

Use contrasting thread to mark cast-on end (otherwise you may get horribly confused later)

Robe: left shoulder

Using straight needles, cast on 20 sts using cable cast-on.

Rows 1–10 Work in st st starting with a knit row.

Row 11 K11, (k2tog, k) three times (17 sts).

Row 12 and all even rows to Row 34 P across.

Row 13 K11, (k2tog, k) twice (15 sts).

Row 15 K9 (k2tog, k) twice (13 sts).

Row 17 K7 (K2tog, k) twice (11 sts).

Row 19 K5 (k2tog, k) twice (9 sts).

Row 21 K3 (k2tog, k) twice (7 sts).

Row 23 K across.

Row 25 K3 (inc1, k) twice (9 sts).

Row 27 K5 (inc1, k) twice (11 sts).

Row 29 K7 (inc1, k) twice (13 sts).

Row 31 K9 (inc1, k) twice (15 sts).

Row 33 K11 (inc1, k) twice (17 sts).

Row 35 K11 (inc1, k) three times (20 sts).

Rows 36–45 Work in st st starting with a purl row.

Cast off (bind off).

Use contrasting thread to mark cast-on end (to avoid aforementioned horror).

Tablet

Using straight needles, cast on 10 sts using cable cast-on.

Work 24 rows in st st starting with a knit row.
Cast off (bind off).

Crown strip

Using straight needles, cast on 18 sts using cable cast-on.
Row 1 K across.
Row 2 P across.
Cast off (bind off).

Crown spikes

Mark seven places evenly across the cast-on side of crown strip with one at each end and the rest in between.
Pick up 2 sts at one end of crown strip you have just knitted.
Rows 1–5 Knit as I-cord.
Row 6 K2tog (1 st).
Cut yarn and thread through last st, knot and thread back into spike to hide end. Repeat six more times for the remaining spikes.

Torch base

Using straight needles, cast on 3 sts.
Rows 1–5 K as I-cord.
Row 6 Inc1 across as I-cord (6 sts).
Row 7 K across.
Row 8 P across.
Row 9 (K, inc1) three times (9 sts).
Cast off (bind off).

Torch flame

Using DPNs cast on 4 sts in gold yarn.
Knit 5 rows as I-cord.
Thread yarn through sts and knot to finish.

Feet (make 2)

Using straight needles, cast on 4 sts.
Knit 10 rows.
Cast off (bind off).

FINISHING

Assembling Liberty

Stuff body, adding optional weight at the bottom if you like. Place small piece of card in the bottom and sew on base. Push pipe cleaner ends of arms into shoulders and use yarn ends to stitch in place.
Place right shoulder robe over right arm (her right, not yours) with cast-on end at the front (I told you to mark it). Sew to the middle of the body. Sew the cast-off (bound-off) end of the right shoulder robe onto middle of the back. Fold left shoulder robe in half with the purl side out, so the sides match up. Sew together 4cm (1½in) of the right sides (sloping side) from the bottom up. Sew together 6cm (2⅓in) of the left sides from the bottom up. Leave the top few cm open for the armhole. Turn right side out.
Pull left shoulder robe over Liberty's head and onto the body. Pull left arm (hers, not yours) through the armhole.

Final touches

Sew on eyes using sewing needle and black thread.
Use green yarn to embroider ears on either side of head and nose in middle of face, by sewing around 2 sts eight times.
Embroider hair by sewing strands from each ear to centre of head – one by one – and moving from the forehead to back of neck on each side.
Sew through 4 strands at the back of the neck ten times to make 'knot' at back of hair.
Sew crown across head from ear to ear with the spikes at the top. You may need to help the spikes stick up by sewing into the bottom of them.
Fold both feet in half. Sew each foot on to bottom of body. Embroider toes by sewing a stitch from the middle of the foot, over the front and back into the underneath, then pulling it tight. Do this twice – once a little to the left and once a little to the right – to form three toes (she's a cartoon Liberty and can get on perfectly well with three toes on each foot).
Fold tablet piece around cardboard and stitch along the edges. Embroider 'July IV MDCCLXXVI' on the tablet.
Sew side seam of torch to make cup.
Sew flame into centre of torch.
Bend right hand to hold torch and bend left arm to hold tablet.
Celebrate Little Lady Liberty's arrival with that Big Appletini she ordered.

CHANGE UP

Little Lady Liberty could be pretty much any world-famous statue you like. Bust out the big arms and beard for Brazil's Christ the Redeemer, hand her a sword for the humongous Mother Russia or go all manly and make Michelangelo's David (using the leg-sewing technique from the Knit New Yorkers pattern). Stitched statues are so much softer than those marble and metal ones, too. Squish a sculpture near you. Go on.

"On the Town"

According to three visiting sailors, prone to burst into song: *'New York, New York, it's a helluva town, the Bronx is up, and the Battery's down.'* And they're right, New York is so packed with cool stuff that you'll never see it all in one visit. But that doesn't mean you ain't gonna try, dammit!

Whether you're zipping uptown for an arty gallery opening dahleeeeeng, or dawdling downtown to eat your weight in dim sum, you can bet dollars to donuts that the weather gods will take their starring roles seriously. NYC's big freeze can turn your regular cup of joe to iced coffee in a New York minute. (In 1934 NYC was a teeth-chattering –13°F. AGH!). Wrap up, or frostbitten bits of you will litter Broadway.

Bust out some city knits to weather the weather: stay snug in the snow with the **Lights, Camera, Action Leg Warmers**, keep your head heated with the **Blockbuster Beanie**, and festoon your four-legged friend in the **Pooch on Parade Poncho** (with Doggy Deely Boppers) for a look that says 'pet party over here'. In your face, NYC weather gods! Blizzard or not, bright lights, big city, here we come.

I recall Central Park in fall...

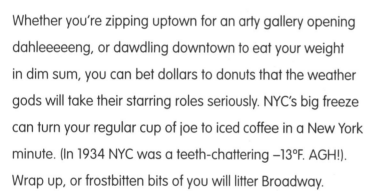

Later, I will poo in your shoes for this, human.

LIGHTS, CAMERA, ACTION LEG WARMERS

Aaaaaaaaaand action! NYC is quite the star of the silver screen. It can be seen strutting its funky, skyscraping, street-tough stuff in hundreds of films. Over 250 features are shot on location in New York each year, and most star Robert DeNiro or Al Pacino.

While conjuring up New York knits, I watched over 80 films to fill my brain with Big Apple ideas. I had lobsters with Annie Hall; got slimed with Venkman, Stanz and Spengler; tried to convince a taxi driver I wasn't talking to him; was made an offer I couldn't refuse; decided I'd have what Sally was having; boogied in flares on a flashing dance floor; got a Cracker Jack Ring engraved at Tiffany's; worried about Rosemary's newest family member; and foolishly agreed to meet Cary Grant at the top of the Empire State Building (hope I make the appointment).

In honour of this celluloid celebration I present to you the Lights, Camera, Action Leg Warmers. Simple to make, marvellously easy to movie up, and red-carpet-ready for a saunter down that crimson runner. That's a wrap! Literally, in the case of your legs.

FIXINGS

Needles
5mm 30cm-long long circular needle (US size 8, 12in long)

Yarn
100g (3½oz) aran (medium) yarn in a colour of your choice (less for shorter and more for longer with fold, natch!)
Optional: Scraps of aran (medium) yarn in other colours for embellishment

Other stuff
Stitch marker
Scissors
Tapestry needle
Bits for embellishment: buttons, beads, bows, ribbons, bottle caps, movie reel, one of Johnny Depp's dreadlocks bought on eBay, sequins, felt, fabric (you get the idea)
Sewing needle and thread

Difficulty rating: Tourist
Size: 50g (1¾oz) makes approx. 30cm (12in) length, with 18cm (7in) diameter unstretched; 45cm (18in) stretched.
Gauge: 26 sts and 24 rows = 10cm (4in) in rib pattern

PATTERN

Leg warmers (make two – unless you're a pirate with a peg leg)

Cast on 50 sts in yarn colour of your choice using the alternate cable cast-on (see The Way of the Knit).

Place marker at first stitch and join to knit in the round (if it's too tight to join, knit one row and then join. You can use the yarn end to sew up the little gap).

(K, P) around in a rib pattern until the piece is as long as you want.

Cast off (bind off) loosely in pattern.

Weave in ends.

Leg warmers don't actually warm your whole leg, do they? Why aren't they called shin and calf warmers?

MUPPETS TAKE MANHATTAN MONSTER LEG WARMERS

Eyeballs (make 2)

Cast on 4 sts in white yarn. Knit 65cm (25½in) as I-cord. Cut yarn and thread through sts pulling tight to close top.

Pupils (make 2)

Cast on 4 sts in black yarn. Knit 65cm (13¾in) as I-cord. Cut yarn and thread through sts pulling tight to close top.

FINISHING

Cut four circles of white felt, approx. 6cm (2½in) wide. Using white thread sew the white I-cord for the eyeball onto the felt in a spiral, starting from the centre. Tuck the end between the cord and felt and sew in to finish. Using black thread sew the black I-cord for the pupil onto the eyeball in a spiral, starting from the centre. Tuck the end under the cord and sew in to finish. Place the legwamer onto something that stretches it out (probably easiest to use your leg) and sew the eyeballs onto each side approx 3.5cm (1½in) from the top using white yarn. You must sew the eyeballs on while leg warmers are stretched, to avoid them becoming too tight when you wear them. Cut eight 2.5cm (1in) triangles from felt and round off one of the points on each to make teeth). Sew four triangles onto the bottom of each legwarmer at the front and on the outside edge. Fold the bottom up to form the 'jaw'. Put them on your legs and go and scare the cat.

Buttons are your friends. There is probably a perfect button in existence for every movie ever made. Go forth and button find.

My NYC Lights, Camera, Action Leg Warmers

The Lights, Camera, Action Leg Warmer designs are made in four film-poster flavours: *West Side Story:* red with black 'fire escape' pattern for star-crossed lovers style; *Ghostbusters:* black with ghostly glowing stripes of the spooky kind; *The Muppets Take Manhattan:* Monster green with white felt triangle teeth and I-cord eyes sewn on for Muppet madness; and *When Harry Met Sally:* glorious, golden, Central Park in fall, hand-dyed yarn based on the movie poster's amazing autumn colours, with a scattering of autumn leaf beads.

Pick your favourite movie poster and ask your friendly neighbourhood yarn dyer to create a yarn inspired by its colours. Cool movie chic and you're supporting local crafty goodness.

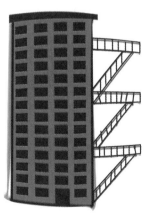

CHANGE UP

In a radical move from the original pattern you can wear your leg warmers as arm warmers. Cast off (bind off) 2 to 4 stitches on the round where you want the thumbhole to be, then cast on the same number on the next round. Easy peasy, lemon squeezy (just don't squeeze lemons while wearing them. You'll get lemon juice everywhere). You could also up the number of stitches and make a giant body stocking. This would be really odd but I'd love to see it.

BLOCKBUSTER BEANIE

Many Hollywood stars spend time in New York pretending to be real people like the rest of us. Spot Dustin Hoffman dunking donuts at The Diner, wonder at Steve Buscemi waiting on line for a chocolate bobka; spy SJP kicking it Carrie-Bradshaw-style in Starbucks; and say 'Oooo! There's Woody Allen!' everywhere (NYC fact: Woody Allen is actually the spirit of New York and can be anywhere at any time. AGH! He's behind you!). Make like a silver-screen star on a day off by knitting up a Blockbuster Beanie, popping on shades and sighing, 'No autographs, please! Can't I just live like a normal person?!', when anyone catches your eye on the subway. Go on.

FIXINGS

Needles
4mm 40cm-long circular needle (US size 6, 15¾in)
4 mm (US size 6) double-pointed needles for decrease (if you can't do magic loop – see The Way of the Knit)

Yarn
50g (1¾in) aran (medium) yarn in a colour of your choice
Optional: small amounts of yarn for embellishments

Other stuff
Stitch marker
Scissors
Tapestry needle
Bits for embellishment: buttons, beads, bows, ribbons, safety eyes, dangerous eyes, beady eyes, golden eyes, hungry eyes, sequins, felt, embroidery thread, fabric (you get the idea)
Sewing needle and thread

Difficulty rating: Tourist
Size: Approx. 46cm (18in) around unstretched. Stretches to fit most heads (if not, add extra sts in twos to keep the pattern)
Gauge: 22 sts and 24 rows = 10cm (4in) in rib pattern

PATTERN

Cast on 88 sts in yarn colour of your choice, place marker at first stitch and join to knit in the round.

Work in k2, p2 rib until hat measures 15cm (6in) for a beanie without fold or 21cm (8¼in) for a beanie with fold.

Crown (if using DPNs you'll need to change to these as work gets smaller)

Round 1 (K2, p2, k2, p2tog) around (77 sts).
Round 2 (K2, p2, k2, p) around.
Round 3 (K2, p2, k2, p) around.
Round 4 (K2, p2tog, K2 p) around (66 sts).

Don't keep measuring every row. It won't make your knitting go any quicker and your tape measure will get tired and cranky.

Round 5 (K2, p, k2, p) around.
Round 6 (K2, p, k2, p) around.
Round 7 (K2, p, k2tog, p) around (55 sts).
Round 8 (K2, p, k, p) around.
Round 9 (K2, p, k, p) around.
Round 10 (K2tog, p, k, p) around (44 sts).
Round 11 (K, p, k, p) around.
Round 12 (K, p, k, p) around.
Round 13 K2tog around (22 sts).
Cut yarn and thread through sts pulling tight to close top.
Darn in ends.

Sometimes while knitting in the round you'll suddenly find you're knitting backwards. That'll teach you to knit while watching a subtitled film.

MUPPETS TAKE MANHATTAN MONSTER BEANIE

Eyeballs (make 2)

Cast on 4 sts in white yarn. Knit 80cm (32in) as I-cord. Cut yarn and thread through sts, pulling tight to close top.

Pupils (make 2)

Cast on 4 sts in black yarn. Knit 80cm (18in) as I-cord. Cut yarn and thread through sts, pulling tight to close top.

FINISHING

Cut two circles of white felt, approx. 7cm (3in) wide.

Using white thread, sew the white I-cord for the eyeball onto the felt in a spiral, starting from the centre.

Tuck the end between the I-cord and the felt and sew in to finish.

Using black thread, sew the black I-cord for the pupil onto the eyeball in a spiral, starting from the centre. Tuck the end under the I-cord and sew in to finish.

Place the hat on something that stretches it out (I used a soft toy) and sew each eyeball onto the hat using white yarn. You must sew the eyeballs on the hat while stretched, to prevent it becoming too tight when you wear it.

Cut six 3cm (1in) triangles from white felt and round off one of the points on each triangle to shape the tip of each 'tooth'.

Sew the triangles onto the outside edge of the hat at the front. Fold the brim up to form the 'jaw'.

Put it on your head and allow yourself a monster dance. You deserve it.

My NYC Broadway Beanies

The Broadway Beanie designs come in the same film-poster flavours as the Lights, Camera, Action Leg Warmers. They can also come in sweet or salt flavours if you add condiments, but then you'd have to wash them.

CHANGE UP

The Blockbuster Beanie can be made little or long depending on how bored you get knitting round and round and round. Knit it really long in orange and white stripes, and you'll resemble one of those steam funnels that stick out of NYC's streets. Make a Blockbuster Beanie to match a pair of Lights, Camera, Action Leg Warmers and admire yourself in shop windows as you walk past them, while pretending that you're looking at whatever the shop is selling.

POOCH ON PARADE PONCHO

Aaaaaaaaaaaoooooooooooo! New York City is home to over one million hairy hounds, and the city's proud collection of canine citizens has it all. There are dog walkers for the lazy, dog runners for the sporty, dog day care for the busy, dog boutiques for the wealthy and eco-friendly dog pampering parlours offering canine choco-lattes and mutt massages.

Listen in at any Central Park doggy drinking fountain, and you'll hear canine kind discussing New York at knee height: dropped hot dog treasure; freshly sprinkled fire hydrants; last night's episode of *Law and Order*; or that cute Pekinese from the apartment opposite.

To celebrate these fine four-legged friends you can stitch them up a spectacular Pooch on Parade Poncho to keep them warm and woolly in the winter, and a set of Doggy Deely Boppers to utterly shame them in front of all their dog friends. Show off your handmade on your hound in the style of the city's partying parades.

FIXINGS

Needles
5.5 mm (US size 9) straight needles
4mm (US size 6) double-pointed needles for I-cord

Yarn
Approx. 100g (3½oz) DK (worsted) yarn in a colour of your choice
10–20g (⅓–⅔oz) DK (worsted) yarn in a colour of your choice for earband
Optional: Small amounts in other colours for accessories

Other stuff
Slightly chilly dog in need of warmth
Tape measure
Somewhere to write measurements that won't get eaten by your dog
Something to write them with
Scissors
Approx. 15cm (6in) of sew-on Velcro (hook side only), 5cm (2in) wide
Sewing needle and thread to match your poncho
Tapestry needle
2 × 30cm (12in) pipe cleaners

Difficulty rating: Gothamite
Size: Sizes are approximate, as dogs are such different sizes. Check which one yours is closest to around the middle: Teeny – 33cm (13in); Small – 38cm (15in); Medium – 43cm (17in); Large – 48cm (19in); Extra-large – 53cm (21in)
For even larger dogs add on 8 sts for each extra 5cm (2in), plus an extra 4cm (1⅗in) to get the right width (the poncho should drape either side of the belly to just below halfway. Too long, and it'll get in the way of walkies.)
Gauge: 16 sts and 16 rows = 10cm (4in) in st st

PATTERN NOTES

First you need to measure your dog. Here are the measurements you need: Back (neck to tail); Head (around head from under chin to just behind ears); Middle (around the middle over the back and under the belly at the thickest part. (The rest of the measurements are taken as you knit the project. Just to make things interesting – measuring a dog while wrangling a WIP is an excellent skill to acquire.)

The Pooch Poncho could be adapted for your cat, too. I'd like to see you try to put it on that flighty feline though.

PATTERN

Main part of poncho

For a Teeny pooch, cast on 18 sts (20 sts for Small/Medium; 24 sts for Large/Extra-large). Work in garter st.
Row 1 Inc1 twice, knit to last 2 sts, inc1 twice (22: 24: 28 sts).
Row 2 K.
Row 3 Inc1 twice, knit to last st, inc1 twice (26: 28: 32 sts).
Row 4 K.
Row 5 Inc1 twice, knit to last st, inc1 twice (30: 32: 36 sts).
Row 6 K.

For Teeny and Small pooches: go straight on to main body, as you already have the right width).

For Medium:
Row 7 Inc1, knit to last st, inc1 (36 sts). Move on to main body.

For Large:
Rows 7–8 Repeat Rows 5–6 once more (40 sts).
Row 9 Inc1, knit to last st, inc1 (42 sts). Move on to main body.

For Extra-large:
Rows 7–12 Repeat Rows 5–6 three times (48 sts). Move on to main body.

Main body
Work in garter stitch from here until the piece measures the same length as your back measurement.

Neck
Teeny, Small, Medium: Knit the first 9 sts, cast off (bind off) 12 (14: 18) sts, knit the last 9 sts.
Large and Extra-large: Knit the first 12 sts, cast off (bind off) 18 (24) sts, knit the last 12 sts.
The work is now split into two sides, which you'll knit separately.

Left neck strap
Row 1 K to last two sts, k2tog.
Row 2 K across.

Row 3 K to last two sts, k2tog.
Here you're going to have a quick measure. Place the coat on the dog's back with the knitting end at your dog's shoulders. Measure from the side you are knitting to halfway around your dog's neck. Add 2–5cm (1–2in) to this measurement (depending on how big your dog is).
Continue to knit that length in garter stitch.
Cast off (bind off).

Right neck strap

Row 1 K, k2tog, knit across.
Row 2 Knit across.
Row 3 K, k2tog, knit across.
Work in garter stitch to the same length as the left side.
Cast off (bind off).

Belly strap (make 1 or 2 depending on how big your dog is)

Cast on 8 (Teeny) 10 (Small/Medium) or 12 (Large/Extra-large) sts with two strands of yarn held together. Work in garter stitch until it is long enough to go from one side of the jacket, pass under the belly and overlap on the other side by about 5cm (2in) (you'll need to put the jacket on the dog and check this as you knit – the fit needs to be snug enough to be secure, but not too tight).
Cast off (bind off).

> Make things fairer by asking your dog what he/she would like you to wear. See how you like it.

FINISHING

Sew a 3cm (1¼in) piece of Velcro to the inside of the cast-off (bound-off) end of the right neck strap.
Sew a 3cm (1¼in) piece of Velcro to the outside of the cast-off (bound-off) end of the left neck strap.
Sew a 5cm (2in) piece of Velcro to the outside of the cast-off (bound-off) end of the belly strap.
Drape the coat over your hound and check where you need to sew the belly strap.
Take the coat off the dog and sew the non-Velcro end of the belly strap to the coat.

Put the coat back on the dog and fasten it to check that it fits.
Take the coat off the dog.
Give your dog a treat. That's the second time she or he has had to put on and take off that coat.
Watch your dog wait for you to put the coat on again – he or she will be expecting it now, clever beast.
Embellish the coat any way you like. Just make sure none of your embellishments get in the way of the dog being comfy in the poncho. It's all about the dog. You're just a human who makes it things.
Put your finished poncho proudly on your hound.
On to the earband!

EARBAND

With yarn held double, cast on 12 sts in chosen colour.
Work in garter stitch until the piece is as long as your Head measurement plus 5cm (2in). Cast off (bind off).

Deely boppers (make two)
Cast on 5 sts in chosen colour on DPNs or circular needle.
Knit 10cm (4in) as I-cord.
Cut 15cm (6in) of yarn and thread through sts. Pull tight to close.

Stars or other shapes (make two)
Cast on 5 sts in chosen colour on DPNs or circular needle.
Knit 30cm (12in) as I-cord.
Cut 15cm (6in) of yarn and thread through sts but do not pull tight yet.

Rabbit ears cord (make two)
Cast on 5 sts in white on DPNs or circular needle.
Knit 20cm (8in) as I-cord.
Cut 15cm (6in) of yarn and thread through sts but do not pull tight yet.

> If your dog won't wear the earband you can wear it yourself. You know you've always wanted your own set of antlers.

Rabbit ears middle (make two)
Cast on 3 sts in pink yarn.
Work in garter st until piece measures 8cm (3¼in).
Cast off (bind off).

FINISHING EARBAND

Fold earband in half lengthways, measure by wrapping around your dog's head to make sure you have at least 5cm (2in) overlap at the ends. Mark the two spots on the folded edge where you want deely boppers or rabbit ears to be placed (they should be on top of the head, in the middle with a space between them). Sew up the ends and the edges of the earband leaving middle 10cm (4in) open.
Bend the last 8cm (3¼in) of the first pipe cleaner into a circle and wind tip back around stem a few times to secure. The circle will sit inside the earband, flat against the dog's head so that the deely boppers stand up.
At the opposite end of the pipe cleaner, fold down 1cm (½in) of tip to get rid of sharp end. Push this end of the pipe cleaner into the earband through the open gap so it comes out of the fold where you want the first deely bopper, star or rabbit ear to be placed.

For deely boppers
Bend the pipe cleaner in half and push the tip of the pipe cleaner back through the fold in the earband, at the same place it came out. Wrap the tip around the stem to secure it (you should be able to do all this through the 10cm (4in) gap you left).
Push the folded length of pipe cleaner into the deely boppers I-cord with the

cast-off (bound-off) end at the bottom. Repeat with the second pipe cleaner. Pull the I-cord tight with cast-off (bound-off) yarn end and use the yarn to sew the bottom of the deely boppers I-cord to the earband. Sew around the two circles of pipe cleaner inside to hold them in place. Sew the gap in the earband closed. Place deely bopper tops on the tip of the pipe cleaner. Use the cast-on yarn end to stitch it in place.

Using stars or other shapes

Repeat the steps above, up to sewing the gap in the earband closed. Push one 30cm (12in) pipe cleaner into each of the 30cm (12in) pieces of I-cord you knit for your shapes.
Bend pipe cleaner into shape of your choice, making sure the two ends meet. For stars bend evenly five times.
Pull the yarn from the I-cord tight and use it to sew the ends of the I-cord together. Leave the tail long. Place a shape on the tip of each pipe cleaner attached to the earband. Use the cast-on yarn end to stitch them in place.

For rabbit ears

Push one 30cm (12in) pipe cleaner into the rabbit ears I-cord with the cast-off (bound-off) end at the bottom.
Bend the pipe cleaner in half and push the tip of the pipe cleaner back through the fold in the earband with 2cm (½in) in between. Wrap the tip around the stem to secure it – (you should be able to do all this through the 10cm (4in) gap you left).
Repeat with the second pipe cleaner. Pull the I-cord tight with cast-off

(bound-off) yarn end and use the yarn to sew the bottom of one side of the rabbit ear I-cord to the earband.
On the other end, thread the cast-on end of the yarn through the I-cord and use the yarn to sew this side of the rabbit ear I-cord to the earband. Repeat for the second ear.
Sew around the two circles of pipe cleaner inside to hold them in place. Sew the gap in the earband closed. Sew pink middle of rabbit ears into middle of each ear.

WEARING THE EARBAND

Sew Velcro onto last 1.5cm (⅔in) of earband on the inside.
Sew Velcro onto first 1.5cm (⅔in) of earband on the outside.
Ask your dog, politely, if he/she'd like to try the earband on. Promise him/her that he/she won't look silly.
Offer him/her bacon if he/she can tell you are lying.

Wrap the earband around your dog's head, securing with the Velcro on the inside first and then the outside. Admire your handsome handmade hound with added deely boppers or your new rabbit that used to be your dog. Dr Moreau, eat your heart out.

CHANGE UP

The Pooch on Parade Poncho can be adapted to celebrate any parade or party that floats your boat. Here are a few ideas:

Star-spangled Beagle: Knit the main coat in red. Knit white stripes to run across the back and a blue square for the top left corner. Sew star buttons or embroider stars onto blue patch. Finish it off with sparkling I-cord stars.

Easter Parade Bunny: Knit with white eyelash yarn or fun fur held together with two strands of DK (worsted) yarn. Add pom-pom to tail area and add rabbit ears to your earband.

Pride Pooch: Knit in colours of the rainbow flag and add happy faces, gender symbols or peace signs to the deely boppers.

Halloween Hound: Knit in black with skull and pumpkin buttons sewn along the coat's edges. Finish off with little knitted spooks skulls on the deely boppers.

Home Turf

Home is where the heart is. Sure, it's only a tiny apartment in among other teeny, tiny apartments, but it's not about size. It's your little bit of the city and you're proud of it. Home is where you wash away the subway grime and pick off the gum stuck to the seat of your pants (curse you, gum-chewing subway swine); it's where you gaze out from your 15th-floor fire escape and breathe in that sweet city smog; where you flush dear departed pets into the city sewers; where you mix the best Mimosa this side of Brooklyn Bridge; and where you have practised the fine art of ordering out so often that you have it down to 30 seconds flat.

Here, in your castle, you need two things: comfort and cocktails. Size doesn't matter here either. New York likes its food big and its cocktails close to hand. These scaled-up and scaled-down stitched stars do both. Invite round the **Big Bad Burger**, the **Huge Hot Dog Cushion** and a sprinkling of tiny **Cocktail Teenies**. Break out the cocktails, pull up a huge fast-food floor cushion and relax.

We're gonna need more ketchup...

Anyone else feeling a bit shaken but not stirred?

BIG BAD BURGER

The humble burger. Whether you have your patty plain or piled up with everything on it, this is the fast-food friend you really can't go wrong with. Stuff a burger in your face and you feel like a king. It's got bread, it's got meat, it's got more bread. What more could you ask for (except more meat, perhaps)?

Stitch a gargantuan Big Bad Burger for your home, and if Godzilla or King Kong arrive for a snack you can fool them long enough to get the hell outta there. Plus there are few better feelings in the world than combining a food and a pillow fight without the mess. Doink someone on the head with a huge purled patty in a stitched sesame seed bun. Go on.

FIXINGS

Needles
Set of five or six 12mm (US size 17) double-pointed needles or 12mm 120cm-long circular needle (US size 17, 47in long)

Yarn
400g (14oz) light brown super chunky (super bulky) yarn for bun
200g (7oz) dark brown super chunky (super bulky) yarn for burger
50g (1¾oz) green super chunky (super bulky) yarn for lettuce
20g (⅔oz) yellow super chunky (super bulky) yarn for cheese
10g (⅓oz) red super chunky (super bulky) yarn for tomatoes
Small amount of thick white yarn for sesame seeds (optional)

Other stuff
Stitch marker
Scissors
Pillows or small single duvet (comforter) for stuffing
Tapestry needle

Difficulty: Yellow Taxicab Driver

Size: Approx. 160cm (65in) around and 65cm (26in) across

Gauge: 7 sts and 12 rows = 10cm (4in) in st st

PATTERN

Top bun

Cast on 24 sts in light brown yarn, holding two strands together.
Divide sts between four or five DPNs or split for magic loop (see The Way of the Knit). Place marker and join to knit in the round.

Round 1 K around.
Round 2 and every even row K around.
Round 3 (K3, inc1) around (30 sts).
Round 5 (K4, inc1) around (36 sts).
Round 7 (K5, inc1) around (42 sts).
Round 9 (K6, inc1) around (48 sts).
Round 11 (K7, inc1) around (54 sts).
Round 13 (K8, inc1) around (60 sts).
Round 15 (K9, inc1) around (66 sts).
Round 17 (K10, inc1) around (72 sts).
Round 19 (K11, inc1) around (78 sts).
Round 21 (K12, inc1) around (84 sts).
Round 23 (K13, inc1) around (90 sts).
Round 25 (K14, inc1) around (96 sts).
Round 27 (K15, inc1) around (102 sts).
Rounds 28–29 K around.

Burger

Change to dark brown yarn.
Round 30 K around.
Round 31 Sl 1 purlwise, p around.
Rounds 32–40. P around.

If presenting your burger to a friend as a gift, try out the traditional New York hunger query: 'Jeet jet?' (Did you eat yet?), before busting out the knitty bun.

Bottom bun

Change to light brown
Round 41 (K15, k2tog) around (96 sts).
Round 42 and every even row Knit around.
Round 43 (K14, k2tog) around (90 sts).
Round 45 (K13, k2tog) around (84 sts).
Round 47 (K12, k2tog) around (78 sts).
Round 49 (K11, k2tog) around (72 sts).
Round 51 (K10, k2tog) around (66 sts).
Round 53 (K9, k2tog) around (60 sts).
Round 55 (K8, k2tog) around (54 sts).
Round 57 (K7, k2tog) around (48 sts).
Round 59 (K6, k2tog) around (42 sts).
Round 61 (K5, k2tog) around (36 sts).
Round 63 (K4, k2tog) around (30 sts).
Round 65 (K3, k2tog) around (24 sts).
Cut 20cm (8in) tail and thread yarn through sts, pull tight to close gap, knot

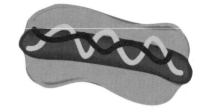

and darn in end.
Stuff with duvet making sure the shape is round.
Using cast-on yarn end, thread it through the first 24 sts, pull tight to close gap, knot and darn in end.

Cheese (make 4)

Cast on 10 sts with a single strand of yellow yarn.
Row 1 K across.
Row 2 and every even row P across.

Take your Big Bad Burger along to the ball game to cushion tiny heinies on those hard plastic seats and give smaller ball fans a bit of a boost.

Row 2 K, k2tog (12 sts).
Row 3 K, k2tog (8 sts).
Cast off (bind off).

FINISHING

Sew lettuce around bun where top bun and burger join.
Sew tomatoes to bun above lettuce where top bun and burger join. Sew both sides and cast off (bind off) end to bun to create the round shape.
Sew cheese to bun below lettuce where top bun and burger join.
Using thick white yarn, embroider sesame seeds on top of bun

Don't stuff your Big Bad Burger with real burger toppings. Seriously that's just wrong.

Row 3 K2tog twice, knit to last 4 sts, k2tog twice (6 sts).
Repeat Rows 2–3 until you have 2 sts. Cut yarn and thread through sts. Darn yarn into edge of piece towards cast-on end and tighten before you knot to stop piece curling up.

Lettuce (make three)
Cast on 60 sts in green yarn.
Row 1 K across.
Row 2 K2 tog across.
Cast off (bind off).

Tomato (make three)
Cast on 18 sts with red yarn using the cable cast-on (see The Way of the Knit).
Row 1 K across.

CHANGE UP
Like a real-life burger you can add anything you like to your Big Bad Burger order. Purl some pickles, make some mushrooms, handmake a handful of jalapeños. You can also turn it into a delicious deli roll or add jam for donutness.

HUGE HOT DOG CUSHION

FIXINGS

Needles
Set of five or six 12mm (US size 17) double-pointed needles or 12mm 60cm-long circular needle (US size 17, 23½in long) for the sausauge and the bun
8mm (US size L11) crochet hook for the mustard and ketchup

Yarn
400g (14oz) pink super chunky (super bulky) yarn for sausage
600g (21oz) light brown super chunky (super bulky) yarn for bun
Small amount yellow super chunky (super bulky) yarn for mustard
Small amount red super chunky (super bulky) yarn for ketchup

Other stuff
Stitch marker
Scissors
Pillows for stuffing
Tapestry needle
Pins

The dirty-water hot dog is a New York institution. Cover him in onions, shower him in mustard or shovel sauerkraut on his meaty form, and deep down he'll still be a hot dog. He'll still be the fast food you hunger for, even when you suspect his innards are made from those peaky-beaked pigeons and slumped staring street dogs you saw hanging about hungrily last week.

So wrong, but so horribly right, the hot dog is one of NYC's finest food fellows, and to celebrate the celebrity sausage in a bun I dedicate this Huge Hot Dog Cushion to every street-corner vendor out there. May the rivers of mustard and ketchup continue to flow, may the onions carry on sizzling and may we never, ever have to see the ingredients list.

Difficulty rating: Yellow Taxicab Driver
Size: Approx. 80cm (36in) long x 65cm (26in) around
Gauge: 7 sts and 11 rows = 10cm (4in) in st st

PATTERN

Sausage

Cast on 40 sts in pink with yarn held double, leaving a 20cm (8in) tail. Divide onto four or five needles or distribute around circular needle for magic loop. Place marker and join to knit in the round.

Work in st st until sausage is 80cm (36in) long.

Cut 20cm (8in) of yarn and thread through sts. Pull tight to close end, knot and darn in end.

Use cast-on tail end to thread through cast on sts.

Stuff Sausage.

Pull cast-on end yarn tight to close end. Knot and darn in end.

> Use cheap stuffing from questionable sources to stuff your Huge Hot Dog Cushion to give it that same mystery meat air that its tiny meaty brethren have.

Weird. You just made a giant sausage. Allow yourself at least three rude jokes and one Twitter picture.

Bun

Cast on 60 sts in light brown with yarn held double, leaving a 20cm (8in) tail.

Divide onto four or five needles or distribute around circular needle for magic loop. Place marker and join to knit in the round.

Work in st st until bun is 55cm (21½in) long.

Cut yarn leaving 20cm (8in) tail.

COMPLETING THE BUN

To make one end of the bun, thread yarn through 30 of the sts and back through the first one you threaded through. Tighten to close and knot. This makes one side of the end of the bun. Thread the yarn through the remaining 30 stitches and back through the first one you threaded through this time. Tighten to close and knot. Darn in end. This makes the second side of the same end of the bun.

Flatten the bun with the two round sides of the bun on the left and right at the closed end.

Sew through top and bottom of the bun lengthways up the middle of bun to make the two sides of the bun.

Stuff each side lightly from the open end (too much stuffing will mean it won't wrap around the sausage).

Close up the other end of the bun in the same way that you made the first.

> Put a small wedding veil on the Huge Hot Dog Cushion, find a sausage dog wearing a bow tie, and take a picture. Ah, l'amour.

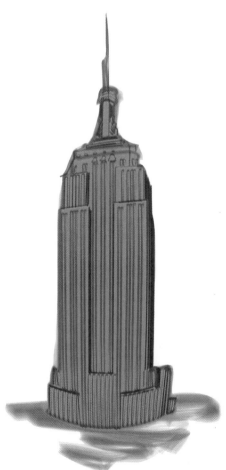

Mustard and Ketchup

For the mustard, use yellow yarn held double, and use a crochet hook to chain 100 sts.

Cut yarn leaving one 15cm (6in) tail and one 120cm (47in) tail. Thread yarns through final sts to close.

Repeat with the red yarn for the ketchup.

FINISHING

Place sausage in centre of bun and sew sides of bun to sausage.

Arrange mustard in a squirty squiggle on top of sausage, using pins to hold in place.

Use 120cm (47in) tail to sew mustard to sausage.

Repeat with the ketchup.

Place your Huge Hot Dog Cushion in the centre of the room and marvel at it.

Go and eat something. You must be starving. Probably not in the mood for a hot dog though.

You could use your Huge Hot Dog Cushion as a dancing partner when you practise for your Saturday Night Fever dance off.

CHANGE UP

It's a giant sausage in a bun.
You decide.

COCKTAIL TEENIES

Cocktail parties are where the rest of the world thinks New Yorkers are all the time – mainly because we wish we were at a NY cocktail party. They're just so damn classy. The only trouble is that, with all the elbow rubbing and air kissing 'mwah', it's hard to keep track of your glass. The social faux pas of drinking from anyone else's glass would be so mortifying you'd never be able to attend a cocktail party again. The drink-sipping shame of it!

Luckily for you, cocktail-party conundrums will be a thing of the past, as here come the Cocktail Teenies! There are martinis, appletinis, dirty martinis, blue martinis, black martinis and dry martinis (which are actually wet). So a few extra teenies won't make much difference now, will they?

Cocktail Teenies hang from cocktail glasses helping you to pick out your hooch from the herd. Target your tipple by adding one of five fun, fibre flavours: Shimmer the Cosmopolitan Star, Sour the Tom Collins Lemon, Sugar the Manhattan Cherry, Pickle the Martini Olive and Quacker the Long Island Iced Tea Duck. Chin chin!

FIXINGS

Needles
Set of four size 2.5mm (US size 1) double-pointed needles or circular needle for magic loop (see The Way of the Knit)
2.5mm (US B1/C2) crochet hook (optional, see Sugar)

Yarn
2g (¹⁄₁₀oz) 4ply (sport) yarn for each cocktail teenie:
Bright yellow for Shimmer
Light yellow for Sour
Red for Sugar
Green with a little red for Pickle
White with a little bright yellow for Quacker

Other stuff
Stitch marker
Stitch holder (for Cosmopolitan)
Scissors
Tapestry needle
Stuffing
Tweezers (optional but helpful when stuffing)
Seed beads for eyes
Sewing needle and black thread
Black embroidery thread (for Pickle)
Craft wire (thick enough to stay in shape once bent and one that won't rust)
Pliers for bending wire (optional)
Silver thread
Cocktail (to hang your Teenie from)
Bar tender (optional, but it'll save you mixing your own cocktails)

Difficulty rating: Gothamite
Size: Approx. 3cm (1¼in)
Gauge: Not important

PATTERNS

Shimmer the Cosmopolitan Star
Star side (make 2)

Cast on 5 sts using bright yellow yarn.
Divide sts between three needles, place marker at start of round and join to knit in the round.

Round 1 Inc1 each st (10 sts).
Round 2 K around.
Round 3 Inc1 each st (20 sts).
Round 4 K.
Row 5 K4 sts and place remaining sts on stitch holder while you work on these four.
Row 6 P2tog twice (2 sts).
Row 7 K across.
Cut yarn with 30cm (12in) tail and thread it through sts.

Sew the yarn back along the point, towards the centre of the star and into the stitch just to the right of the next stitch you're going to work. You're going to use it to knit the next point.
Use the yarn to knit the next four stitches off the stitch holder.
Rep rows 6 and 7.
Rep the process of sewing the yarn back towards the centre of the star.
Rep with the next four stitches, and the next four, until all five points have been made.

> Teenies are fiddly. So very fiddly. Don't cry. It will be over soon.

FINISHING

Sew both halves of Cosmopolitan the Star together, knit sides out.
Stuff the points of the star lightly as you go (this is where the tweezers come in handy).
Poke some stuffing into the centre just before sewing the star closed.
Sew on eyes, using a sewing needle and black thread.

Sour the Tom Collins Lemon

Cast on 3 sts in light yellow yarn.
Row 1 Inc1 across (6 sts).
Divide sts between three needles, place marker at start of round and join to knit in the round.
Round 2 K around.
Round 3 (K, inc1) around (9 sts).
Round 4 K around.
Round 5 (K2, inc1) around (12 sts).
Round 6 K around.
Round 7 (K3, inc1) around (15 sts).
Rounds 8–10 K around.
Round 11 (K3, k2tog) around (12 sts).
Round 12 K around.
Round 13 (K2, k2tog) around (9 sts).
Round 14 K around.
Round 15 (K, k2tog) around (6 sts).
Round 16 K around.
Stuff.
Round 17 K2tog around (3 sts).
Cut yarn, thread through sts and pull tight to close end.

FINISHING

Pinch Sour the Tom Collins Lemon into shape so ends are pointy.
Sew on eyes, using a sewing needle and black thread.

Sew tiny black cross onto bottom of Pickle using black embroidery thread. Sew on eyes, using a sewing needle and black thread.

Quacker the Long Island Iced Tea Duck

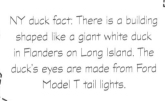

Body

Cast on 6 sts.

Divide sts between three needles, place marker at start of round and join to knit in the round.

Round 1 K around.
Round 2 (K, inc1) around (9 sts).
Rounds 3–5 K around.
Round 6 (K2, inc1) around (12 sts).
Round 7 K around.
Round 8 K around.
Round 9 (K3, inc1) around (15 sts).
Rounds 10–11 K around.
Round 12 (K3, k2tog) around (12 sts).
Round 13 (K2, k2tog) around (9 sts).
Round 14 (K, k2tog) around (6 sts).
Stuff.
Cut yarn, thread through sts and pull tight to close end.

Head

Pick up 6 stitches on top of body at the larger end.
Knit 4 rows as I-cord.
Cut yarn, thread through sts and pull tight to close end.

NY duck fact: There is a building shaped like a giant white duck in Flanders on Long Island. The duck's eyes are made from Ford Model T tail lights.

FINISHING

Using yellow yarn, embroider beak of Quacker the Long Island Iced Tea Duck by first sewing through front of head from left to right three times. Then sew around these stitches eight times by going in at the top and out at the bottom to make the beak stick out. Sew an eye either side of head, using a sewing needle and black thread.

Pickle the Martini Olive

Cast on 6 sts in green yarn.
Divide sts between three needles, place marker at start of round and join to knit in the round.
Round 1 (K, inc1) around (9 sts).
Round 2 K around.
Round 3 (K2, inc1) around (12 sts).
Rounds 4–7 K around.
Round 8 K2, k2tog around (9 sts).
Round 9 K around.
Round 10 (K, k2tog) around (6 sts).
Stuff.
Cut yarn, thread through sts and pull tight to close end.

FINISHING

Sew 'pepper stuffing' into top of Pickle the Martini Olive using red yarn. .

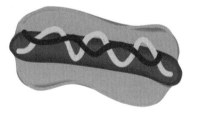

Sugar the Manhattan Cherry

Body

Cast on 6 sts.

Divide sts between three needles, place marker at start of round and join to knit in the round.

Round 1 (K, inc1) around (9 sts).
Round 2 K around.
Round 3 (Inc1, k, inc1) around (15 sts).
Round 4 K around.
Round 5 (K, inc1, k, inc1, k) around (21 sts).
Round 6 K around.
Round 7 K around.
Round 8 (K, k2tog, k, k2tog, k) around (15 sts).
Round 9 K around.
Round 10 (K2tog, k, k2tog) around (9 sts).
Round 11 K around.
Round 12 (K, k2tog) around (6 sts).
Stuff.
Cut yarn, thread through sts and pull tight to close end.

Stem

Cast on one st in green yarn.
Knit 15 rows (or chain 15 sts with 2.5mm (US B1/C2) crochet hook).
Cut yarn, thread through st and pull tight to close end.

Leaf

Cast on 2 sts in green yarn.
Row 1 Inc1 twice (4 sts).
Row 2 Sl1, k across.
Row 3 Sl1, k across.
Row 4 Sl1, inc1 twice, k (6 sts).
Rows 5–9 Sl1, k across.
Row 10 Sl1, kt2og twice, k (4 sts).
Row 11 Sl1, k across.
Row 12 Sl1, k across.
Row 13 K2tog twice (2 sts).
Cut yarn, thread through st and pull tight to close end.

FINISHING

Using green yarn, sew stem to Sugar the Manhattan Cherry, and sew leaf to stem.
Sew on eyes, using a sewing needle and black thread.

When you put eyes on a Teeny and it blinks up at you, be warned that several knitters have been known to fall wildly in love. Don't look a Teeny directly in the eyes unless you're ready to make that commitment.

HANGING YOUR TEENIES

Cocktail Teeny hooks

First things first, put down your knitting needles. Go on. Now grab your wire and cut an 8cm (3in) length for each hook you want to make. If you're worried about sharp ends, you can add an extra 0.5cm (¼in) to each end and bend it over to round the ends off. Holding one end of the wire curl it around your pliers (or a pencil or large knitting needle) so it's roughly the shape of a lower-case 'e'.

That's all there is to it. You now have your Cocktail Teeny hooks.

> Pretend your Teeny is your best Sex and the City gal-pal by hanging your Teeny from a coffee cup, tapping loudly on your laptop in a coffee shop and loudly telling your Teeny about a disastrous date you had the night before.

Take your hook and tie the Teeny to the very front of the 'e'.

Pop your Teeny onto the edge of a cocktail glass, cup of cwafee or that refreshing glass of homemade lemonade you just bought from the street vendor with the hook hand and the grimace (and which tastes a little odd, but you're too scared to return it). Watch your Teeny dangle. Isn't it cute? Awwwww.

Thread your Teenies

Before you begin, hold your Teenies in your hand and admire them. Squeeeeeeeee!

Cut about 8cm (3in) of silver thread and tie a knot in one end. Thread this strand onto a tapestry needle.

Sew the thread into the Teeny and out of the top of the Teeny's head. Make sure you pull the thread hard enough to bring the knot inside the Teeny, so it doesn't show.

CHANGE UP

The Cocktail Teenies are as changeable as their ingredients. Like teeny Broadway wannabes, these blinky-eyed diddy dancers could be used for anything: beads, earrings, keyrings, charms or festive decorations. Stick them on slides or bands and wear them in your hair. Squish them into a piñata and party when it pops and peppers people with purly pals. The role you cast for your Cocktail Teenies is up to you. You're gonna make those schweethearts schtars!

Wild New York

"City Critters"

New York City is a pretty wild place and it is home to some pretty wild creatures – but let's leave the NY humans aside for a minute. There are four-legged and even six-legged citizens sharing this skyscraper shadowed space. That skittering and scampering under the honk-honking of the gridlocked traffic; that munch-crunching coming from the all-you-can-eat global feast that is restaurant garbage cans; that hungry splish-splashing in the depths of the sewers; and that mysterious shadow that appears to be climbing up the outside of the Empire State Building…

New York's city critters are everywhere. You just have to know where to look.

Introducing four of the Big Apple's wild woolly wanderers: humongous and hairy, **Smash the Angry Ape** (who happens to bear a striking resemblance to King Kong); slinky and street smart, **Scram the Alley Cat**; cute and cuddly and not at all icky, **Scuttle the Cockroach**; and starving and smiley, **Snap the Sewer Alligator**.

SMASH THE ANGRY APE (KING KONG)

FIXINGS

Needles
Pair of 3.5mm (US size 4) straight needles

Yarn
40g (1⅓oz) black DK (worsted) yarn for body, limbs and head
40g (1⅓oz) black fuzzy (eyelash) yarn for body, limbs and head
8g (¼oz) grey DK (worsted) yarn for feet and hands

Other stuff
Scissors
Tapestry needle
2 × 30cm (12in) black pipe cleaners
Stuffing
Safety eyes
Good supply of bananas (optional)

Prepare to be amazed! Prepare to be astounded! Men hold onto your hats and ladies hold onto your men! You're about to knit the greatest thing your eyes have ever beheld. He was a woolly king and a god in the world he knew, but now he comes to New York as a stitched super star! Ladies and gentlemen I give you Smash, the Eighth Woolly Wonder of the World!

Ah. He looks a little angry. Well, you'd be angry too if you didn't have any pants pockets to put your MetroCard in. Uh-oh. He's coming this way.

Does anyone have a giant banana?

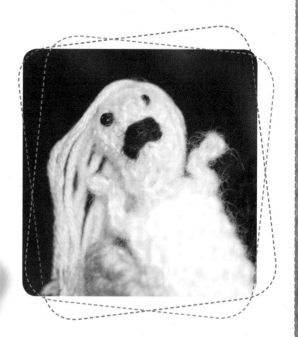

Difficulty rating: Tourist
Size: An impressive 22cm (8½in) tall
Gauge: Not important

PATTERN NOTES

You make Smash's fur by holding the DK (worsted) yarn and fuzzy black (eyelash) yarn together. To save getting tangled it's easier to wind them both into one ball of yarn before you start.

PATTERN

Head

Holding two strands of yarn together, cast on 15 sts in black and fuzzy black yarn.

Rows 1–6 K across.
Row 7 (K, k2tog, k2) three times (12 sts).
Row 8 K across.
Row 9 K2tog across (6 sts).
Row 10 K across.
Row 11 K2tog three times (3 sts).
Cut yarn, thread through sts and pull tight.
Use tail to sew up sides of piece to create a bowl shape for the head.

> Eyelash yarn is hideous to knit with because you can't see your stitches. Where are they!?!??! This is because eyelash yarn was invented by demons. Fact.

Body

Holding two strands of yarn together, cast on 24 sts in black and fuzzy black yarn.
Knit 18 rows.
Cut yarn, thread through sts and pull tight to join top together.

Sew seam along side to create body leaving the bottom open.

Legs (make 2)

Holding two strands of yarn together, cast on 10 sts in black and fuzzy black yarn.
Knit 18 rows.
Cast off (bind off) and cut a 20cm (8in) tail.
Sew long sides together to make a tube for each leg.

Arms (make 2)

Holding two strands of yarn together, cast on 10 sts in black and fuzzy black yarn.
Knit 20 rows.
Cast off (bind off) and cut a 20cm (8in) tail.

Sew long sides together to make a tube for each arm.

Face

Cast on 8 sts in grey yarn.
Rows 1–6 Work in st st starting with a knit row.
Row 7 K2tog across (4 sts).
Row 8 P across.
Row 9 Inc1 across (8 sts).
Row 10 P across.
Row 11 K across.
Cast off (bind off).
Fold the larger part of the face in half and sew the sides together to form the bottom half of the face. Leave the top half flat.

Hands (make 2)

Cast on 8 sts in grey yarn.

Work 12 rows in st st, starting with a knit row.

Cut yarn, thread through sts and pull tight to join top together.

Sew up side seams, knit sides together, leaving the bottom open.

Turn right side out (you might need to poke a pen in there to help you do this).

Feet (make 2)

Cast on 7 sts in grey yarn.

Rows 1–6 Work in st st starting with a knit row.

Row 7 K, inc1, k3, inc1, k (9 sts).

Row 8 P across.

Row 9 K, inc1, k5, inc1, k (11 sts).

Row 10 P across.

Row 11 K, k2tog, k5, k2tog, k (9 sts).

Rows 12–17 Work in st st starting with a purl row.

Cast off (bind off).

Fold in half with knit sides together and with the cast-on and cast-off (bound-off) ends together.

Sew up the side of the foot leaving the cast-on and cast-off (bound-off) ends open.

Turn right side out.

Stuff foot.

Sew up back of foot.

Using grey yarn, sew two stitches into front of each foot to create toe shapes.

FINISHING

Make legs

Fold one pipe cleaner in half (making sure you fold the tips over to prevent sharp ends).

Push each half of the pipe cleaner into a leg so you can see it sticking out of the bottom, and with the folded part sticking out of the tops of the legs.

Push one foot onto one end of the pipe cleaner sticking out of the bottom of the leg and sew foot into place using black yarn.

Repeat with second foot.

Stuff legs around pipe cleaner.

Add body

Push second pipe cleaner through top of body, from left to right, so each end sticks out where an arm will be.

Stuff body.

Push leg section into body section and sew tops of legs onto bottom of body using black yarn.

Make arms

Bend each end of the pipe cleaner to make a loop at the end (this forms the shape of the paws).

Push pipe cleaner ends through arm tubes so the loops stick out of the arms.

Sew arms to body using black yarn.

Push a hand onto each pipe cleaner loop and sew in place using black yarn.

Make head

Sew head onto top of body.

Add safety-eye backs to flat part of face (hold them up to face to check they're in the right place).

Sew face onto head using grey yarn, making sure the folded part is at the bottom of the face.

Embroider nostrils using black yarn. Challenge to an arm wrestle. You probably won't win.

Stitch a Scream Queen

Knit Smash a lady to love. Download a free pattern for a Stitched Scream Queen at www.stitchcraftcreate.co.uk.

CHANGE UP

Smash isn't the only man-shaped monster out there. You can use your knitty skills to turn him into many more mythical beasts. Use some funky brown fur to turn your big ape into a yarny yeti or find a flurry of snow-white fluff to make him the most abominable snowman the world has ever known.

SCRAM THE ALLEY CAT

MRAOW! Who strikes fear into the tiny furry hearts of the radioactive rats in the subway? Who has more fleas than you've had pancake breakfasts? Who is pointy-eared king of the trashcan city? There can be only one contender: Scram the NYC Alley Cat.

Scram is a slinker among the shadows and an expert climber of fire escapes. He peers in at pampered penthouse pussycats and shakes his tatty-eared head at their pudgy features. He's a lean, mean feline fellow with the city at his paws and he doesn't need no pesky humans to fill his belly come dinner time. Though he wouldn't mind the end of that hot dog if you're not going to finish it. Hold the mustard.

Difficulty rating: Gothamite
Size: 11cm (4in) tall
Gauge: Not important

FIXINGS

Needles
Set of four size 3.5mm (US size 4) double-pointed needles or circular needle for magic loop (see The Way of the Knit)

Yarn
10g (⅓oz) orange DK (worsted) yarn for head, body and legs
Small amount of black DK (worsted) yarn for nose

Other stuff
Stitch marker
Stuffing
30cm (12in) orange pipe cleaner for neck
Scissors
Black thread for whiskers
Sewing needle
Seed beads for eyes
Saucer of milk (optional)

PATTERN

Head and body

Cast on 3 sts in orange yarn.
Row 1 Inc 1 three times (6 sts).
Divide sts between three needles, place marker at start of round and join to knit in the round.
Round 2 K around.
Round 3 Inc1 around (12 sts).
Round 4 K around.
Round 5 Inc1 twice, k2, inc1 four times, k2, inc1 twice (20 sts).
Round 6 K around.
Round 7 Inc1 twice, k6, inc1 four times, k6, inc1 twice (28 sts).
Round 8 K around.
Round 9 Inc1 twice, k10, inc1 four times, k10, inc1 twice (36 sts).
Rounds 10–12 K around.
Round 13 K2tog twice, k10, k2tog 4 times, k10, k2tog twice (28 sts).
Round 14 K around.
Round 15 K2tog twice, k6, k2tog 4 times, k6, k2tog twice (20 sts).
Round 16 K around.
Round 17 K2tog twice, k2, K2tog 4 times, k2, K2tog twice (12 sts).
Stuff head and shape into oval.

Round 18 K around.
Round 19 K2tog around (6 sts).
Rounds 20–22 K around.
Round 23 Inc1 around (12 sts).
Round 24 K around.

If you can't find a pipe cleaner that is the right colour, try wrapping one in the same yarn you are using to knit so that it doesn't show through your stitches.

Round 25 (K, inc1) around (18 sts).
Round 26 K around.
Round 27 K around.
Round 28 (K2, inc1) around (24 sts).
Rounds 29–31 K around.
Round 32 K2tog around (12 sts).
Round 33 K around.
Round 34 K around.
Push about 6cm (2⅓in) of pipe cleaner into head to support neck (make sure you fold over the tips to prevent sharp ends).
Stuff body.
Cut yarn, thread it through remaining sts and pull tight to close body.

Front paws (make two)

Cast on 2 sts in orange yarn.
Push sts to other end of needle.

Drop your fluffy feline from a fire escape to see if he lands on his feet. Go on... No, not really! Jeez, you're so mean!

Knit 10 rows as I-cord (see The Way of the Knit).
Row 11 Inc1 each stitch as I-cord (4 sts).
Row 12 Knit as I-cord.
Cut yarn, thread through sts and pull tight.

Back paws (make two)

Cast on 2 sts in orange yarn.
Push sts to other end of needle.

Knit 15 rows as I-cord.
Row 16 Inc1 each stitch as I-cord
(4 sts).
Row 17 Knit as I-cord.
Cut yarn, thread through sts and pull
tight.

Ears (make 2)
Cast on 5 sts in orange yarn.
Rows 1–8 Work in st st, starting with a
knit row.
Cut yarn, thread through sts and pull
tight.

Tail
Cast on 2 sts.
Knit 12 rows as I-cord.
Cut yarn, thread through sts and pull
tight.
Thread yarn end down through middle
of tail and pull to make kink in tail.

FINISHING

Sew top of front paws at either side of
neck to make shoulders, and at the feet
so that they face forwards.
Sew top of back paws either side of
body at the bottom, and sew feet just
in front facing forwards. The leg should
make an upwards loop to form the knee.
Sew ears onto top of head. If you feel
like making your moggie authentically
urban you can snip and sew one ear
slightly wonky to give him that street-
fighter look.
Sew tail at back of body.
Embroider nose by sewing the first stitch
into three stitches across the middle of
the face with black yarn. Sew four or five
more stitches through the same three
stitches, pulling them a little tighter each
time to form a triangular nose.

Sew on three whiskers each side of
nose, using a sewing needle and black
thread (knot the thread, pass it through
the back of the head, pull the knot
inside and leave the thread sticking out
of the front to form whisker).

Use the same needle and thread to
sew on eyes.
Check your mangy moggie for fleas.
You'd be surprised how fast those
things appear.

CHANGE UP
Scram is one of many flavours of feline. Since cats come in all sorts
of colours you can change your yarn and your needle size to make
a whole host of crazy city cats. You can even break out the mad
mohair to make a puffed-up Persian or slip something silky on your
needles to make a slinky Siamese. Tabby stripes can be embroidered
on, if colourwork scares the fur off you.

SCUTTLE THE COCKROACH

FIXINGS

Needles
Pair of 3.5mm (US size 4) needles
3.5mm (US E4) crochet hook

Yarn
8g (¼oz) brown DK (worsted) yarn for shell, legs and feelers
8g (¼oz) mustard DK (worsted) yarn for face and underbelly

Other stuff
Scissors
Tapestry needle
Safety eyes
Stuffing
Fabric glue
30cm (12in) brown pipe cleaner
Roach motel for bug relaxation (optional)

'AAAAARRRRRRRRRGGGGGGGGGGGHHH! I saw it! It went under the refrigerator! It was all feelers and feet and it was staring up at me with those freaky insect eyes! Ewwwwwwwwww!' This is the sad cry that Scuttle the Cockroach has to live with every day of her life. Just because she has a hard shell, it doesn't mean that a roach doesn't have feelings too. New York is her city just as much as it is yours. She's ever so polite and only comes out when its dark so you won't be offended by her hideous beetle face. She'd never walk across your face when you sleep – well, maybe just that one time. Can't you show a little bug some love?

Difficulty rating: Tourist
Size: Approx. 9cm (3½in) from back end to nose (if roaches had noses)
Gauge: Not important

PATTERN

Shell and face

Cast on 3 sts in brown yarn.
Row 1 P across.
Row 2 K, m1, k to last st, m1, k (5 sts).
Row 3 P across.
Row 4 Repeat row 2 (7 sts).
Row 5 P across.
Row 6 Repeat row 2 (9 sts).
Row 7 P across.
Row 8 Repeat row 2 (11 sts).
Row 9 P across.
Row 10 Repeat row 2 (13 sts).
Row 11 P across.
Row 12 Repeat row 2 (15 sts).
Rows 13–22 Work in st st starting with a purl row.

> When the nuclear zombie apocalypse comes, only cockroaches and zombies will survive. I know whose side I'd rather be on.

Change yarn to mustard colour.
Row 23 K across.
Row 24 P across.
Row 25 K, k2tog, k to last three sts, k2tog, k (13 sts).
Row 26 P across.
Row 27 K, k2tog twice, k3, k2tog twice, k (9 sts).
Row 28 P across.
Row 29 K, k2tog, k3, k2tog, k (7 sts).
Row 30 P2tog, p3, p2tog (5 sts).
Cut yarn leaving 20cm (8in) tail, thread through sts and pull tight.

Underbelly

Cast on 2 sts in mustard yarn.
Row 1 K across.
Row 2 K, m1, k (3 sts).
Row 3 K across.
Row 4 K, m1, k, m1, k (5 sts).
Row 5 K across.
Row 6 K, m1, k to last st, m1, k (7 sts).
Row 7 K across.
Row 8 Repeat row 6 (9 sts).
Row 9 K across.
Row 10 Repeat row 6 (11 sts).
Row 11 K across.
Row 12 Repeat row 6 (13 sts).
Row 13 K across.
Rows 14–21 K across.
Row 22 K, k2tog, knit to last 3 sts, k2tog, k (11 sts).
Row 23 K across.
Row 24 Repeat row 22 (9 sts).
Row 25 K across.
Row 26 Repeat row 22 (7 sts).
Row 27 K across.
Row 28 K2tog, k3, k2tog (5 sts).
Row 29 K2tog, k, k2tog (3sts).
Cut yarn, thread through sts and pull tight.

Antennae

Cast on 1 st.
Rows 1–8: K (or use 3.5mm crochet hook and chain 18 sts)
Cut yarn, thread through sts and pull tight.

> Cockroaches can live for a whole month without food but only a week without water. So keep Scuttle hydrated.

FINISHING

Using brown yarn, sew brown part of shell to underbelly.

Press safety eyes into face (check you have them where you want them before you snap the backs on. They're not coming back out).

Stuff body.

Using mustard yarn, sew face part of shell to underbelly adding a bit more stuffing before you sew it shut.

Using brown yarn, sew around and around the middle stitch of the shell from back to front to show two wings. You can also embroider where the shell and face meet to define the line there as well.

Avoid paying the bill in an expensive restaurant by placing Scuttle on the table towards the end of the meal and wailing like a banshee. Just remember to share the doggy bag with her when you get home.

Lightly coat the antennae in glue to stop them from curling too much. You can do this by putting a blob of glue onto each one and smoothing it with your fingers. Leave them to dry (it should only take a couple of minutes). Sew antennae onto head either side of the face where it meets the shell.

Cut pipe cleaner into three 10cm (4in) sections. Bend the tips of each part to prevent sharp ends.

Push the pipe cleaners through the body to make six legs, three on either side. (If you can't find brown pipe cleaners wrap yarn around another colour. Use glue to hold ends in place and wrap yarn around and around to cover the whole part that is showing. Sew yarn into body to secure.)

Resist temptation to call the exterminator.

Place Scuttle on your head and wear her as a fascinator. It's a look that says 'insect chic'.

CHANGE UP

If you don't think Scuttle is pretty enough, you could turn her into lovely nine-spotted New York ladybug by knitting her in red and black. You can also make all manner of beautiful beetles using shiny yarns to make the shell or by adding bright buttons and sequins. You could even add some wicked knitted jaws and make your very own stitched stag beetle. Or add round glasses and long hair to make a John Lennon beetle. Or should that be Beatle?

SNAP THE SEWER ALLIGATOR

FIXINGS

Needles
Pair of 3.5mm (US size 4) needles

Yarn
15g (½oz) green DK (worsted) yarn for upper body
15g (½oz) yellow DK (worsted) yarn for underbelly
10g (⅓oz) red DK (worsted) yarn for inside mouth
Small amount of white DK (worsted) yarn for teeth

Other stuff
Scissors
Stitch holder
Tapestry needle
Stuffing
Seed beads for eyes
Sewing needle and black thread
Safety gloves to stop your finger being bitten off (optional)

Down in the belly of NYC is a shadowy world of tunnels, caverns and sewer pipes that stretches a mind-boggling 6,600 miles. In the darkest corner of this world lurks Snap the Sewer Alligator. There are rumours of alligators in New York's sewers as far back as the 1920s, but Snap knows they'd already moved on from the sewers and were working in speakeasies selling moonshine to unsuspecting humans, making them much easier to eat.

Snap is a born and bred New Yorker. He claims his great grandpa was flushed down an apartment toilet by none other than Lucille Ball in an unaired episode of *I Love Lucy* called 'Lucy gets Snappy'. With that mouth full of teeth, who would want to argue?

Difficulty rating: Yellow Taxicab Driver
Size: 18cm (7in) long from nose to tail tip
Gauge: Not important

PATTERN

Upper body

Cast on 4 sts in green yarn.

Row 1 K across.

Row 2 and every even row to Row 26 P across.

Row 3 K, m1, k2, m1, k (6 sts).

Row 5 K, m1, k, m1, k2, m1, k, m1, k (10 sts).

Row 7 K across.

Row 9 K2, k2tog, k2, k2tog, k (8 sts).

Row 11 and every odd row to Row 17 K across.

Row 19 K2, m1, k, m1, k2, m1, k, m1, k2 (12 sts).

Row 21 K2, m1, k, m1, k, m1, k4, m1, k, m1, k, m1, k2 (18 sts).

Row 23 K across.

Row 25 K4, k2tog twice, k2, k2tog twice, k4 (14 sts).

Row 27 K5, k2tog twice, k5 (12 sts).

Row 28 P4, k, p2, k, p4.

Row 29 K4, p, k2, p, k4.

Row 30 P4, k, p2, k, p4.

Row 31 K4, p, k2, p, k4.

Row 32 P4, k, p2, k, p4.

Row 33 K4, p, k2, p, k4.

Row 34 P2, k8, p2.

Rows 35–38 Repeat rows 31–34.

Rows 39–42 Repeat rows 31–34.

Rows 43–46 Repeat rows 31–34.

Row 47 K2, k2tog, p, k2, p, k2tog, k2 (10 sts).

Row 48 P3, k, p2, k, p3.

Row 49 K, k2tog, p, k2, p, k2tog, k (8 sts).

Row 50 P across.

Row 51 K, k2tog, k2, k2tog, k (6 sts).

Rows 52–58 Work in st st starting with a purl row.

Row 59 K, k2tog twice, k (4 sts).

Row 60 P across.

Cut yarn, thread through sts and pull tight.

Underbelly

Cast on 4 sts in yellow yarn.

Row 1 K.

Row 2 and every even row to Row 42 P across.

Row 3 K, inc1 twice, k (6 sts).

Row 5 and every odd row to Row 11 K across.

Row 13 K, inc1, k2, inc1, k (8 sts).

Row 15 K, inc1, k4, inc1, k (10 sts).

Row 17 K, inc1, k6, inc1, k (12 sts).

Row 19 K across.

Row 21 K, k2tog, k6, k2tog, k (10 sts).

Row 23 K, k2tog, k4, k2tog, k (8 sts).

Row 25 and every odd row to Row 35 K across.

Row 37 K, k2tog, k2, k2tog, k (6 sts).

Row 39 K across.

Row 41 K across.

Row 43 K, k2tog twice, k (4 sts).

Rows 45–50 Work in st st starting with a knit row.

Cut yarn leaving a long tail, thread through sts and pull tight.

Legs (make 4)

Cast on 3 sts in green yarn.

Rows 1–4 Knit as I-cord.

Put 2 sts on stitch holder.

Knit 3 rows into remaining stitch to make first toe.

Thread yarn through st and cut 20cm (8in) tail.

Knot yarn and use tapestry needle to sew tail back down toe to base of foot again.

Use yarn to knit 3 rows into the next stitch on the holder to make second toe.

Repeat the last two steps with the last stitch on the holder to make third toe and darn in yarn end.

Inside mouth

Cast on 4 sts in red yarn.

Row 1 K.

Row 2 and every even row to Row 22 P across.

Row 3 K, inc1 twice, k (6 sts).

Row 5 and every odd row to Row 11 K across.

Row 13 K, inc1, k2, inc1, k (8 sts).

Row 15 K, inc1, k4, inc1, k (10 sts).

Row 17 K, inc1, k6, inc1, k (12 sts).

Row 19 K across.

Row 21 K, k2tog, k6, k2tog, k (10 sts).

Row 23 K, k2tog, k4, k2tog, k (8 sts).

Rows 24–32 Work in st st starting with a purl row.

Row 33 K, k2tog twice, k (6 sts).

Row 34 P, p2tog twice, p (4 sts).

Cast off (bind off).

> Amuse yourself during quiet periods at work by screaming wildly while staggering about with Snap attached to your nose. Hours of fun. Use a broken red biro to add authentic blood.

FINISHING

Using green yarn, sew the underbelly to the upper body to approx. 7cm (2¾in) from head on both sides.

Stuff the body up to the mouth.

Using green yarn, sew the mouth section to the inside of the mouth area on the upper body.

Stuff the top of the mouth lightly.

Using green yarn, sew the mouth section to the inside of the mouth area on the underbelly. Lightly stuff it before completely sewing shut.

Using white yarn, embroider teeth along top and bottom edges of mouth.

Sew legs on either side of body at back and front.

Sew on eyes, using a sewing needle and black thread.

Count your fingers to check you've not lost any in the making process. If you have try looking inside Snap's mouth. He's always hungry.

> Make several Snaps and place the whole bunch near an open manhole to simulate a tiny alligator attack. Be careful not to fall in. Real alligators think you taste like chicken.

CHANGE UP

Turn Snap into a crafty crocodile by adding a few more rows to his nose to make it a little longer and adding a longer tooth on each side (a crocodile's fourth tooth on each side along the bottom sticks up over their lips so you can see them both even when their giant jaws are shut).

"Green Guerrilla Knitting

Picture New York back in 1973: Big hair, huge collars, flared trousers and a group of sneaky citizens creeping out of their homes to create something subversive from New York's muddy mess. In a derelict private lot in NYC's Bowery Houston area, the first recorded guerrilla garden was stealthily seeded.

Guerrilla gardening's roots are firmly planted in the unloved areas of New York City. Sure the flowers of covert horticulture have bloomed worldwide from London to Sydney, but New York's Green Guerillas (back then they only had one 'r' in guerrilla) were there from the get go.

The **Blooming Bug** and the **Woolly Wildflower** combine nature, knitting and a large helping of naughtiness – in 'green graffiti yarnstorming'. They are designed to encourage you and your fellow Gothamites to get out there and spread the green glee for all to see. These simple patterns can blossom into something seriously smile-inducing… or at least a nice salad.

BLOOMING BUG

This little critter is the greenest knit that ever there was. He's a handmade hero when it comes to cleaning up New York's areas of neglect. He's packing pollen and ready to get out there on the streets, to bring a bit of knitty nature to places in need. Upcycled from pesky plastic bags, the Blooming Bug holds just enough soil to make a graffiti garden wherever you leave him, and he brings the cute in case people don't approve of his flowery ways.

Stitch up this guerrilla gardening soldier, fill him with budding blooms and release him into New York's cold concrete corners. You can plant a pack of posies in your local playground, fancy up fire-escape railings with a whole hive of handsome handmade herb holders and combat urban decay with a swarm of intrepid insect insurgents.

Difficulty rating: Tourist
Size: Approx. 12 x 10cm (4¾ x 4in)
Gauge: 14 sts and 16 rows = 10cm (4in) in st st

FIXINGS

Needles
Pair of 6mm (US size 10) straight needles

Yarn
Two average-sized plastic bags in different colours
One small white or clear plastic bag for eyes

Other stuff
Good scissors
Large tapestry needle (for sewing up and embroidering with plarn)
Patience
Square of plastic bag for lining
Small potted plant
Cable ties
The guts to go out there and guerrilla garden

FINISHING

Fold in half so the cast-on ends and cast-off (bound-off) ends are together, with knit sides facing. Sew up the sides using plarn and a large tapestry needle. Turn right side out.

Use a contrasting plarn to embroider spots and stripe.

Cut two 7cm (2¾in) lengths of plarn and knot one end of each four times to create antennae. Sew them into place at the top of the head.

Use white or clear plastic plarn to embroider each eye by sewing around 2 sts 10 to 15 times. Use coloured plarn to embroider a pupil for each eye. Line the bottom of your Blooming Bug with a square of plastic bag to prevent all your soil from being washed out when it rains. It'll make it easier for it to retain water, too.

Pop your potted plant out of the pot and into the mouth of the waiting bug. My, but it looks pretty.

Put your shoes on. You're off into the wilds of New York.

PATTERN NOTES

You'll first need to make the plarn (plastic bag yarn).

1 Flatten out your plastic bag into a neat rectangle.

2 Fold your plastic bag in half lengthways and in half again.

3 Cut the handles and bottom off your plastic bag.

4 Chop your bag into strips 2cm (¾in) wide.

5 Pull out the strips and lay two loops end to end, overlapping slightly. We'll call them loop A and loop B.

6 Pull right end of loop A up through loop B, then feed the left end of loop A through its right end.

7 Pull both loops to tighten the knot, securing them together.

8 Continue to add new loops in the same way, over and over, then wind your ball of plarn.

PATTERN

Cast on 15 sts in the colour of plarn you want to use for the head.

Rows 1–7 Knit in st st starting with a knit row.

Change to second colour of plarn.

Rows 8–32 Knit in st st staring with a purl row.

Change back to first colour of plarn.

Rows 33–39 Knit in st st starting with a knit row.

Cast off (bind off) loosely.

RELEASING BLOOMING BUG INTO THE WILD

Finding a happy home

Take your bug out into the streets of New York and choose somewhere for him to live. It's best to pick a neglected nook that you pass by often (on your way to work, school or that regular meeting with your hot Latin lover) so you can keep a beady eye on him and keep his blossoms blooming. It might be tempting to pepper somewhere slightly scary with your plarn pals in the hope of spreading some green grins, but do be careful: marching into crime central with flowery friends for all might not be the best plan.

Installing your insect

Blooming Bugs can be cable-tied to almost anything you can wrap a tie around: chain-link fences, railings, fence posts, parking meters, street signs and people who stand still for too long. The number of cable ties you need will depend on what you are attaching your bug to. You will need to use at least two to three ties so they fasten around the lip of the bug at the back. This is the strongest part, and will also keep your bug upright. (If one cable tie is too short, you can thread two together to make a longer one. Just push a couple centimetres of the end of the second tie into the holder of the first).

Checking up

Once up, you'll need to stop by your bug to keep him blooming. Carry a bottle of water (a NYC must anyway) to give him a sprinkle if it hasn't rained in a while (especially in summer), and find out what he's been up to. You might find others have been checking up on him too. You'd be surprised at the nurturing nature a lonely plant can bring out in people.

Losing a stitched soldier

Sometimes your Blooming Bug will suffer tragedy. He'll either end up going home with an admirer or suffering a sadder fate. Just remember that this is wild New York you are releasing him into, and the handmade happiness he brings is worth all that selfless stitching. You can always make another one, and another, and another, until people are so tired of taking them down that your insect infestation gains victory. Have heart – you're a green graffiti knitter and you'll yarnstorm whatever the weather.

CHANGE UP

If you're too nervous to release your Blooming Bug into the wild, you can always fasten it to your fire escape to give it some fresh air. The beauty of the Blooming Bug is that it is a purly plarn pocket that can be used to hold anything. Hang one on your bathroom door to keep the soap safe, stick your sponge in one at the kitchen sink or make a really HUGE one, attach it to a balloon and float away on it. Not sure that last one will work but wouldn't it be amazing if it did?

WOOLLY WILDFLOWER

Listen up. Word on the street is you've been a little selfish with your knitting. Louis here tells me you've been keeping all that fine stitched swag to yourself. Wearing it around town like you're some woolly wise guy. You're a real piece of work, you know that? Where's the respect? New York is one big family, and if you ain't part of the family you're no one.

We think you and your knitting better get with the programme and start sharing. Now this here is a pattern for a genuine Woolly Wildflower, and you and this pattern are gonna get friendly, see? The beauty part is that you make two pieces: one Woolly Wildflower that you leave in the wind; and a seed bomb for the wise guy who steals your wildflower, along with a little message to share the goods with the city. Your payola, my friend, is a warm fuzzy feeling of giving something to make someone else's day. It's a green-graffiti knitting offer they can't refuse, capisce?

Difficulty rating: Tourist
Size: Approx. 35cm (14in) tall
Gauge: Not important

FIXINGS

Needles
Pair of 4mm (US size 6) straight needles

Yarn
Small amount of bright green DK (worsted) yarn for stem
Small amount of bright-coloured DK (worsted) yarn for petals
Small amount of bright-coloured DK (worsted) yarn for centre of flower

Other stuff
Scissors
Large bowl or tub for mixing
Spoon for stirring
Cardboard tag
6cm (2⅓in) piece of clear plastic bag to wrap your seed bomb in
Sticky tape
40cm (15in) length of strong wire (thick enough to stand straight on its own)
Pliers for bending wire (optional)
Tapestry needle
2 x seed beads for eyes
Sewing needle and black thread
The guts to go out there and graffiti yarnstorm (Eek!)

Ingredients for seed bomb
1 part seed mix (preferably wild flower seeds or seeds of flowers that are native to your area – no exotic seeds, please; you're trying to help nature, not start a plant vs plant war)
1 part compost/potting soil
5 parts clay powder (you can buy this from art stores or online)
1 part water
(Optional 1 teaspoon of cayenne pepper or chilli powder to deter hungry seed-munching beasts)

PATTERN NOTES

The basic idea is that you knit and make the Woolly Wildflower, the label and the seed bomb. Then you put them all together and release them into the wild for a fellow New Yorker to steal and be inspired by. One Woolly Wildflower might not make much difference, but if enough of them hit the streets NYC will be a flowerful fiesta… in more ways than one.

This woolly wildlife is inspired by the street art of Michael de Feo who has painted graffiti flowers all over the world.

PATTERN

Stem

Cast on 5 sts in bright green yarn.
Knit as I-cord until your cord measures 30cm (12in).
Cut yarn, thread through stitches but don't pull tight yet.

Petals

Cast on 5 sts in yarn colour of your choice.
Knit as I-cord until your cord measures 65cm (25½in).
Cut yarn leaving a 20cm (8in) tail and thread through sts. Pull tight and knot.

Centre

Cast on 4 sts in yarn colour of your choice.
Knit as I-cord until your piece measures 10cm (8in).

Cut yarn leaving 15cm (6in) tail and thread through sts. Pull tight and knot.

MAKING A SEED BOMB

1 Mix the seeds and compost.
2 Stir in the clay powder.
3 Add water slowly as you mix (trying to avoid lumps) until your mixture is about the same consistency as modelling clay.
4 Get your hands in there and knead the ball of muddy stuff to make sure it's one big lump (that's a technical term). This makes sure the smaller bombs hold together long enough to survive being thrown and landing on unknown ground, ready for their seedy mission.
5 Make the giant lump into lots of small seed bomb lumps by pinching bits off and rolling them into balls about 4cm (1½in) in diameter. (It doesn't have to be exact. You're a guerrilla! You live outside the rules!) If they start to crumble, add a bit more water.
6 Put the seed bombs somewhere dry for 24–48 hours.
7 Grab your tag and write something similar to this on it: 'Hello fellow New Yorker. This Woolly Wildflower is for you. In return for taking it, you must pass the sharing forward by releasing the attached seed bomb into the wild. Please throw it somewhere with soil and sunshine that needs a little colour'. (You can spell colour without the 'u' if you're feeling less British than me).
8 Pop your seed bomb into a piece of clear plastic and tape it to the back of the tag.

FINISHING

Bend the top 3cm (1in) of the wire to make a small loop.
Bend the bottom 5cm (2in) of the wire to make a larger loop.
Push the small loop into the open end

of the flower stem and feed it all the way up, making sure it doesn't pop out of any of the stitches on the way. The easiest way to do this is to hold the cord straight as you feed in the wire. The 5cm (2in) loop should tuck into the end.

Pull the cord closed around the bottom of the stem. Sew the end through the cord and the loop inside a few times and then knot it securely.

Sew the petals on to the top of the stem making five loops.

Sew the centre cord on to the stem in a circle.

Using a sewing needle and black thread, sew the seed beads on to the centre to make eyes.

With the remaining 10cm (4in) of yarn still attached to the bottom of the stem, thread it through the hole in the tag. Bada bing! You have a Woolly Wildflower and its seed-bomb friend ready to be released into the city.

MAKING THE DROP

You can install your Woolly Wildflower anywhere at all. Poke a hole in the ground (I use an old pair of scissors) and 'plant' it, wedge it between the crack in a brick wall or wrap it around a railing. It's up to you. Just make sure it's where people can see it, and that the label and seed bomb remain firmly attached.

Don't get into trouble. If someone official asks you what you're up to, you can explain (people usually find graffiti knitting charming). If they still don't like it, take your wildflower and run away! Take a picture. A picture means your Woolly Wildflower moment will be

immortalised forever. Plus you can upload it to Planet Whodunnknit at www.whodunnknit.com and show the world.

Check back to see if your wildflower went walkies. If it's still there in two weeks and is looking a bit grisly you might want to try somewhere else. Was that abandoned alleyway such a good idea? And has it been nibbled by something?!

Read Richard Reynold's book *On Guerrilla Gardening*. Richard is an inspiring green graffiti pioneer and his book explains how covert garden craft can change the world.

CHANGE UP

The basic Woolly Wildflower can be used to make many other objects. Stick on a stitched star to conjure up a magic wand, add a handmade woolly moustache for a that much-coveted 'moustache on a stick look' or use the I-cord-over-wire method to cosy your car ariel (or someone else's - that'll confuse them).

The Way of **The Knit**

You are about to turn from a humble non-knitter into a crazed yarn-flinging ninja of the knit. People will stop and stand slack-jawed at your splendiferous stitching, your gorgeous garter stitch and your purling prowess. All you need to do is learn to make these little loops and Bob's your uncle, you're a real live knitter. (Your uncle doesn't have to be called Bob in order for you to be a knitter.)

> Abbreviations for techniques:
>
> LN – Left-hand needle
>
> RN – Right-hand needle

LIGHTS. CAMERA. CAST ON.

Casting on, making the first stitches of your project, is the opening titles to your knitting. A good cast-on sets the stage for some blockbuster knitting action and means you're well on your way to a knit you can proudly shove in the faces of other people and shout 'Look what I made!'

There are many different breeds of cast-on stitches. Some methods are better for certain projects and some are just fancy. If you want your knitting to be exactly like the pattern, use the suggested cast-on. If you're not too fussed, use your favourite cast-on and see what happens.

The slip knot

The slip knot is the start of every knitting project you'll ever make. Learn it well. The slip knot is your friend.

Follow these pictures to make your slip knot and your first cast-on stitch. Make sure you have at least a 15cm (6in) tail of yarn on your slip knot. Annoying as it might be, it is the only thing that will stop your knitting from unravelling later.

Pull the ends of the yarn to tighten your knot. Don't pull it too tight, though. You're going to have to get both your needles into that little loop in order to knit. Awwwww. Just look at it. All lonely there on the needle. It needs friends. On to the cast-on!

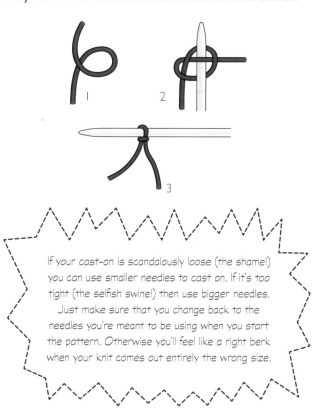

If your cast-on is scandalously loose (the shame!) you can use smaller needles to cast on. If it's too tight (the selfish swine!) then use bigger needles.
Just make sure that you change back to the needles you're meant to be using when you start the pattern. Otherwise you'll feel like a right berk when your knit comes out entirely the wrong size.

Knitted cast-on

This fairly loose cast-on uses the basic knit stitch and two needles. She's not the prettiest or neatest of cast-ons but, trust me, she is the easiest and best cast-on to start with when you're a newbie. Honest, guvnor.

1 Take two needles and make a slip knot about 15cm (6in) from the end of the yarn on one needle. Hold this needle in your left hand.

2 Insert the RN from left to right (we call this 'knitwise') into the loop on the LN. Your needles should make a cross, with your RN behind your LN. You should be able to hold both these needles with your left hand, leaving your right hand free to wrangle the yarn.

3 Wrap the yarn around and under the tip of the RN (anticlockwise from back to front). It should end up between your RN and LN.

4 Slide the RN down, catch the wrapped yarn with your needle tip and pull it out of the front of the loop. You should end up with a loop on your RN.

5 Pull out the new loop a bit and then slip it onto the LN by inserting the LN underneath the loop and up through the middle.

6 Remove the RN from the loop and tug the yarn to tighten it, but not too much. Tight stitches are evil to knit with. You want your stitches nice and relaxed. You will now have two stitches on the LN.

7 Repeat the above using the new 'stitch' you just made. Keep doing this until you have as many stitches as you need.

8 You've cast on. Feel free to look a bit smug.

Cable Cast-On

The cable cast-on is a good one to swoon over. He's neat and has a firm edge that is also elastic. He's perfect for a bit of rib stitch or when you're looking for a straight-line start (such as with Squishy Empire State). You can also use him to cast on stitches in the middle of a row.

Repeat steps 1–6 of the knitted cast-on.

7 Insert the RN between the two stitches on the LN and wrap the yarn around the tip in the same way as the knitted cast on. Pull the yarn back through between the two stitches and place it on the LN, as in step 5. Repeat until you have cast on enough stitches.

To cast on extra stitches mid-row, work step 7 only, working the first stitch between the next two stitches already on the LN.

Alternate Cable Cast-On

This does all the fabulous things that the cable cast-on does but makes a pingy stretchy ribbed edge, too.

For first two stitches repeat steps 1–7 of cable cast-on.

8 Insert the RN between the two stitches on the LN from back to front.

9 Wrap the yarn around the tip from left to right.

10 With the tip of the RN push the yarn back between the two stitches, pull it out and place it on the LN.

Repeat these stitches alternately (needle from front to back, then from back to front) until you have cast on enough stitches.

Thumb cast-on

This cast-on uses one needle and is the simplest and quickest way of casting on. It can be a bit baggy though, and tends to leave you with long bits of yarn between stitches when you start to knit, causing some new knitters to go into a rabbit-in-car-headlights stare. It might be best to use it once you know what you're doing.

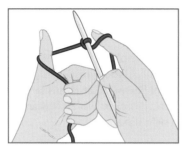

1 Take one needle, make a slip knot about 15cm (6in) from the end of the yarn and slip it onto the needle. Hold this needle in your right hand.

2 Wrap the yarn from the ball around your left thumb from front to back. Hold it in your palm with your other fingers.

3 Insert the needle upwards through the strand of yarn on your thumb and slip the loop into the needle.

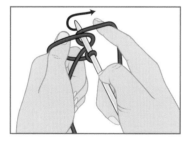

4 Pull the yarn to tighten (not too tight!) and repeat until you've cast on enough stitches.

KNIT, PURL, RULE THE WORLD

You're here at last. The moment you've been waiting for. After this you'll be a knitter. From here on in, it's a slippery slope into feeding your filthy yarn habit by selling precious family heirlooms and knitting under your desk when you're meant to be working.

Knit stitch

The best part is that if you used the knitted cast-on, you almost know how to knit already. You're going to be doing a whole lot of knit stitch, so get comfy with her. Sure, she may seem a bit confusing at first, but practise and treat her right and she'll make a nifty knitter of you. It's going to be the start of a beautiful friendship.

Start off holding the yarn at the back of the work (the side facing away from you).

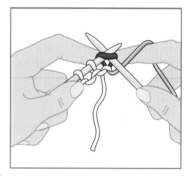

1 Place the needle with the cast-on stitches in your left hand, and insert the RN into the front of the first stitch on the LN from left to right. Your needles should make a cross with your RN behind your LN. You should be able to hold both these needles with your left hand, leaving your right hand free to wrangle the yarn.

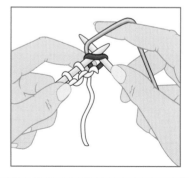

2 Wrap the yarn around and under the RN (anti-clockwise from back to front). It should end up between your RN and LN.

3 Slide the RN down, catch the wrapped yarn with your needle tip and pull it out of the front of the loop. You should end up with a loop on your RN.

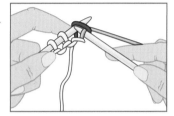

4 Slide the stitch you just looped through off the LN. Go on. Pop it off the end. You might need to shuffle the other stitches up a bit to make it easier. This has formed one knit stitch on the RN.

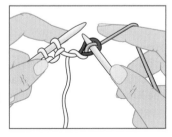

5 If it's loose, tug the yarn to tighten the stitch, but not too much. You will now have knit one stitch on the LN with the rest still on your RN.

6 Repeat the above by using the next stitch on the LN and inserting your needle in the same way. Keep doing this until all the stitches on the LN have been transferred to the RN. Yup, even that last one.

7 Sit back and admire your first knitted row. It's really rather marvellous. Allow yourself a bite of cake.

8 Now swap your needles over. Your RN becomes your LN and your LN becomes your RN. Repeat all the steps above all over again. Then again and again and again until your knitting is long enough or your arms drop off.

> Important: Before you begin the next knit row, always make sure your yarn comes from the bottom of the needle to the back of the work. It must be at the back before you begin to knit. If you mysteriously get an extra stitch and your knitting is beginning to look triangular, it's because your yarn was pulled over the top of the needle. You're not prey to knitting gremlins. You just have your yarn in the wrong place.

Purl stitch

The purl stitch is a robust and manly rounded stitch. He's the reverse of the knit stitch and is a bit like knitting backwards. With the purl stitch you can make all kinds of knitting madness. He's a bit trickier than the knit stitch and some people dislike him for it. Once you get the hang of tangoing with the purl though, you're laughing. He's a reliable chap and knitting would be a sad and one-sided world without him. Once you know how to purl, you know **everything**.

Start off holding the yarn at the front of the work (the side facing you). I really, really mean it when I say HOLD IT IN FRONT. That means for **every** purl stitch. If you don't, monsters will eat you and your knitting will be in a right state, too.

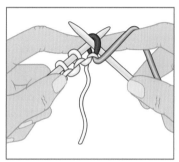

1 Place the needle with the cast-on stitches in your left hand, and insert the RN into the front of the first stitch on the LN from right to left. Your needles should make a cross, with your RN in front of your LN. You should be able to hold both these needles with your left hand, leaving your right hand free to wrangle the yarn.

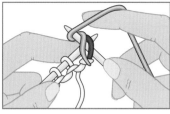

2 Wrap the yarn around and over the RN (anti-clockwise from back to front). It should end up between your RN and LN.

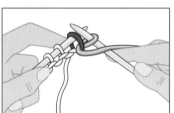

3 Slide the RN down, catch the wrapped yarn with your needle tip and push it out of the back of the loop. You should end up with a loop on your RN.

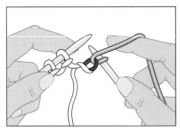

4 Slide the stitch you just looped through off the LN. Go on. Pop it off the end. You might need to shuffle the other stitches up a bit to make it easier. This has formed one purl stitch on the RN.

5 If it's loose, tug the yarn to tighten the stitch, but not too much. You will now have purled one stitch on the LN with the rest on your RN.

6 Repeat the above by using the next stitch on the LN and inserting your needle in the same way. Keep doing this until all stitches on the LN have been transferred to the RN. Yup, even that last one.

7 You purled! You're on your way to stitch sagacity.

> Learn what your stitches look like. Knit stitches resemble little Vs and purl stitches look like little bumps. An easy rhymey way to remember them is that purls curl and knits don't.

I THINK IT'S STILL MOVING! FINISH IT OFF!

So I lied about you knowing everything there was to know. You still need to learn to cast off (bind off). Otherwise, you'll just keep knitting and knitting, unable to stop, gradually fading away under a huge pile of endless stitches where you'll survive on cake crumbs until they can dig you out.

Casting off loops the stitches together so they can't unravel, no matter how much they might want to, and secures them to finish your project. It's a satisfying 'Byeeeee!' to your knit. Free your project from the needles!

Important: Don't cast off too tightly by pulling your yarn for all you're worth after you cast off each stitch. You'll end up with a tight and narrow end.

Cast off Knitwise

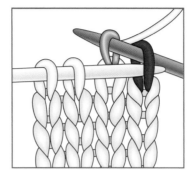

1 Knit the first two stitches. Insert the point of the LN into the front of the first stitch on the RN. You might need to tug the stitches down a bit from below to do this if your knitting is quite tight. Do it. They won't mind. They'll be too busy being excited about the cast-off.

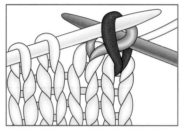

2 Lift the first stitch on the RN over the second stitch and off the needle. Be careful not to push both stitches off.

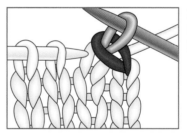

3 One stitch is left on the RN. The other is cast off. Hooray!

4 Knit the next stitch on the LN, so there are again two stitches on the RN. Lift the first stitch on the RN over the second stitch, as in step 2. Repeat this process until one stitch is left on the RN. Cut the yarn (leaving a length long enough to sew or weave in) and pass the end through the last stitch. Slip the stitch off the needle and pull the yarn end to tighten it.

Cast off purlwise

Casting off purlwise is exactly the same was casting off knitwise, just with purls instead of knits. Easy.

Cast off in pattern

If you've got a pattern in your knit – a bit of rib, a smattering of moss stitch, or something fancier – then you really should cast off in pattern to keep the edge nice and stretchy. It's not rocket science. Just knit the knit stitches and purl the purl stitches.

Ta daaah! In your sweaty paws you should now hold your very own first knitted square. Admire its beauty. Its handmade wobbly stitches and mysterious holey bits. Feel yarn-flavoured pride at your creation and fear not: you will learn to perfect your knit in time.

MORE, YOU SAY? OTHER USEFUL STITCHES AND STUFF

Garter stitch and stocking stitch

Ooh la la! Garter stitch and stocking stitch (stockinette stitch) are a couple of racy little numbers. They're rows of knitting that build up to form your fabric. Allow me to introduce the two main sisters of stitch patterns.

Garter stitch (g st) is made up of rows of knit knit knit knit knit knit (you get the idea). She's got wavy ridges on the front and the back, and both sides look the same. Garter stitch lies down flat and makes a thicker fabric than stocking stitch. She's the simplest stitch pattern to do. Get the hang of garter and you won't even need to look at your knitting to knit it.

Stocking stitch (st st) is made up of rows of knit then purl then knit then purl then knit (again you get the idea). She's a sleeker and neater stitch, and makes a dazzlingly lovely fabric with all the knits on one side (the right side) and all the purls on the other (the wrong side). The one thing about stocking stitch is that she never lies flat. She's a curly minx and will always roll up at the edges, no matter what you do. Stocking stitch is best for sleeves and jumpers, but is not so great for scarves.

Instructions for stocking stitch in patterns can be written like this:

Row 1 K.
Row 2 P.

Or, alternatively: Work in st st (1 row k, 1 row p), beg with a k row.

To remember which stitch sister is which, remind yourself that blushing brides normally wear one garter (just the knit stitch) and two stockings (knit and purl stitch).

Rib stitch

Rib stitch is the annoying half-brother of garter and stocking stitch. He's a mix of the two. He's the stretchy bit at the end of sleeves, collars and cuffs that keeps your ends from flapping. He's ever so satisfying to admire once you've got him right.

Rib stitch is made up of knits and purls. It can be done in any combination of numbers across a whole row; for example, rows of two knits and two purls.

Important rib stitch stuff

• The knit and purls must line up under each other. If you see a knit stitch, knit it; if you see a purl stitch, purl it.

• Pass your yarn between your needles when you change from knit to purl. This is the most important thing in the world when you are doing rib stitch. If you forget to do this, your rib stitch will be rubbish. Utter, utter rubbish. So sad.

THE WOBBLY WORLD OF INCREASING AND DECREASING

Once you get sick of squares, you'll probably want to start getting into shapes. Most newbie knitters have horror at the thought of stepping away from the comfort of plain knit and purl, but shaping is simple. You just remove or add stitches as you go. It's really easy to do, doesn't take long to learn and probably won't make you swear out loud as much as some of the more fiddly stitches you might want to learn later. Be brave and throw yourself into a bit of shaping. Go on!

Increasing Stitches

Make 1 (m1)

Make 1 (m1) magically creates a new stitch in between two existing stitches. It uses the horizontal thread that lurks between the stitches. Twisting the stitch prevents a hole appearing in your knitting and makes your increase practically invisible. I said 'practically'. There are people who will be able to see it, the eagle-eyed swines.

To twist m1 to the left

1 Work to the place you want to increase and insert the LN under the horizontal strand between the next two stitches from front to back.

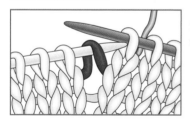

2 Knit this loop through the back to twist it.

To twist m1 to the right

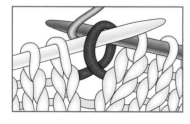

1 Work to the place you want to increase and insert the LN under the horizontal strand between the next two stitches from back to front.

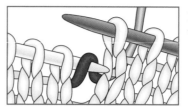

2 Knit this loop through the back to twist it.

Increase 1 (inc1)

Inc1 does what it says on the tin (increases the number of stitches by one). It is most often used at the edges of a knitted piece. Do it neatly and it's virtually invisible in the pattern of stitches. Do it badly and people will point and laugh. Try to keep an even tension as you add stitches; when you're knitting into the same stitch twice, it's easy to make it tight, and frown lines cause wrinkles in old age.

Inc1 on a knit row

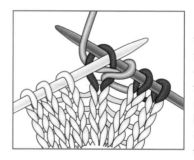

1 On a knit row, knit the first stitch on the LN in the usual way, but instead of sliding the stitch off the LN as you would normally do, knit into the back of the same stitch (still keeping the yarn at the back of the work).

2 Slide the stitch off the LN. You now have two stitches on the RN and have created a stitch. Ooooh. It's like magic!

Inc1 on a purl row

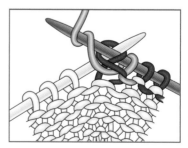

1 On a purl row, purl the first stitch on the LN in the usual way, but instead of sliding the stitch off the LN as you would normally do, purl into the back of the same stitch (still keeping the yarn at the front of the work).

2 Slide the stitch off the LN. Voila! An extra stitch.

Decreasing stitches

Knit two stitches together (k2tog)

The k2tog and you will get to know each other very well. It's the bog-standard method for decreasing, and it does show in the fabric as well as making it narrower.

1 Knit to where you want to decrease and insert the RN knitwise through the next two stitches on the LN.

2 Knit these two stitches together as if they were one stitch.

Purl two stitches together (p2tog)

1 Purl to where you want to decrease and insert the RN purlwise through the next two stitches on the LN.

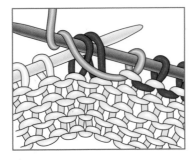

2 Purl these two stitches together as if they were one stitch.

GOODBYE SEAMS, HELLO CIRCULAR KNITTING

It is a well-known fact among all knitters that sewing up seams is as close to pure evil as crafting gets. Wouldn't it be fabulous to have no seams to sew up at all? Seamless knitting is possible through the wonder that is circular knitting.

Flat knitting is knitted in rows that go back and forth and wander from one needle to the other. With circular knitting, you work round and round rather than in rows. At the end of the round, you just carry on knitting without having to swap your needles over. This makes a tube-like piece of knitting. It really is the lazy knitter's dream.

Circular knitting is friend of small tubular knits like gloves, hats, socks and sleeves. It can be used for bigger things too, like laptop socks, scarves and giant man-eating pythons.

There are two ways to get your circular knit on: double-pointed needles (DPNs) or the fantastical beast that is the magic loop.

Double-pointed needles (DPNs)

Useful for self-defence in case of a zombie apocalypse, DPNs are also great for circular knitting, from teeny-tiny tubes to giant socks of doom. They're fairly easy to use, although they look more complicated than they are. They are good for using on the tube to scare people away from sitting next to you. You will generally use a set of four DPNs; three needles hold the stitches and you work with the fourth.

1 Cast on the number of stitches required on to one needle. It's best to use the knitting-on method, as the cast-on stitches need to be fairly loose.

2 You then need to divide the stitches evenly between three needles. (Note that when dividing stitches between needles, they should not be too far apart. If the stitches are stretched when the needles are joined, use a shorter needle.)

3 Make sure that the cast-on edge is facing inwards and is not twisted. If you don't do this you'll have twisted knitting. And I don't mean in the heavy metal sense.

4 Bring the three needles together to form a triangle. Place a stitch marker to indicate the end of the round (slip this on to the next needle for every round).

5 Taking your fourth needle, knit the first cast-on stitch, pulling the yarn tight to avoid creating a gap between the first and third needle.

6 Knit the remaining stitches from the first needle. The first needle is now empty and becomes the working needle.

7 Knit the stitches from the second needle onto the working needle. The second needle is now empty and becomes the working needle.

8 Knit the stitches from the third needle onto the working needle. You have now completed one round. Impressive.

9 Continue working in this way to produce a piece of tubular fabric.

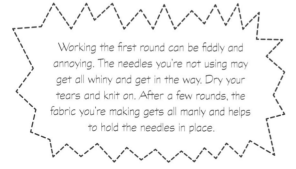

Working the first round can be fiddly and annoying. The needles you're not using may get all whiny and get in the way. Dry your tears and knit on. After a few rounds, the fabric you're making gets all manly and helps to hold the needles in place.

The magic loop

I heart magic loop more than any other knitting technique. It's not everyone's cup of tea (milk and no sugar, please), but once you and magic loop are one, nothing can stop you. You're invincible. (Please don't test this out by jumping off anything.)

Magic loop lets you use the marvel that is a circular needle (two needles joined by a thin cord) to knit any sized tube at all. Literally any size. We're talking so small you have to squint to see it. My, how I love magic loop.

1 Using a long circular needle (100cm/40in is probably best), cast on the number of stitches you need.

2 Slide them to the cable part of the circular needle.

3 Count to the halfway point in your total number of stitches and pull a section of cable out between the stitches. It doesn't need to be exactly half if the number of stitches isn't even.

4 Slide the divided stitches back up the needles.

5 Pull the RN through so half the stitches are on the cable and your RN is free to move where it pleases.

6 Join the stitches to form a ring by knitting the first half of the stitches from the LN onto the RN. You should end up with stitches on both needles again. Make sure your stitches aren't twisted before you do this.

7 Pull the cable to slide the second half of the stitches onto the LN and pull the RN through so half the stitches are on the cable. Your RN is free again.

8 Knit the second half of the stitches.

9 Repeat steps 7 to 8 for each row.

Magic loop works best if you make sure you pull the first stitch quite tight. You'll end up with ladders otherwise. Tiny people will be able to climb up your knitting and steal stuff.

ZUT ALORS! CONTINENTAL KNITTING!

Continental knitting is often faster, involves fewer elbows flying about, and looks really cool. The main difference is that you hold your yarn in your left hand instead of your right, while the needle scoops the yarn as it goes with a flick of the finger. Some people prefer continental knitting to the usual knit. It's worth a go just to boast to people about being multi-knitual.

Continental Knit

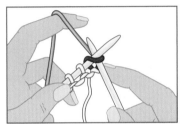

1 Hold the needle with the cast-on stitches in your left hand and the yarn over your left index finger. Insert the RN into the front of the stitch from left to right.

2 Move the RN down and across the back of the yarn.

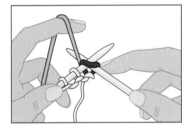

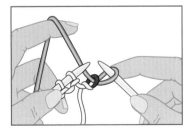

3 Pull the new loop on the RN through the stitch on the LN, using the right index finger to hold the new loop if needed.

4 Slip the stitch off the LN. One continental knit stitch is completed. Mon dieu!

Continental purl

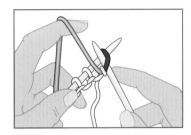

1 Hold your yarn in front of the work. In front, I say!

2 Hold the needle with the cast-on stitches in your left hand and insert the RN into the front of the stitch from right to left, keeping the yarn at the front of the work.

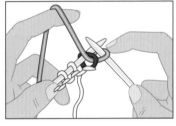

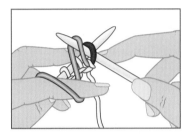

3 Move the RN from right to left behind the yarn and then from left to right in front of the yarn. Pull your left index finger down in front of the work to keep the yarn taut.

4 Pull the new loop on the RN through the stitch on the LN, using your right index finger to hold the new loop if needed.

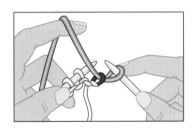

5 Slip the stitch off the LN. Return the left index finger to its position above the needle. One continental purl stitch is completed. Sacré bleu!

I CORD. YOU CORD. WE ALL CORD I-CORD.

The 'I' in I-cord stands for 'idiot'. It's called Idiot-cord because it's so easy to make that even the most feeble-minded fibre-flinger can rustle some up. I-cord can be used for all kinds of things from decorating a lovely bit o' knitting to using as a lasso to capture those winged machete monkeys that keep attacking you on the way to the Emerald City.

1 On a circular or double-pointed needle, cast on a small number of stitches. Fewer than five works best.

2 Push the stitches to the other end of the needle and turn the needle, so the first stitch you'll knit is the first one you cast on.

3 Knit the stitches, making sure you pull the yarn tight for the first stitch.

4 Shove the stitches to the other end of the needle.

5 Repeat steps 3 and 4 until the I-cord is the desired length.

6 Balance I-cord on top lip and pretend you have a droopy moustache. We've all done it.

THE BORING HORROR OF GAUGE SWATCHES

Do you want your knit to be just like the pattern in shape and size like an eerie knitted clone? I'm sorry to report that you're going to have to switch on your brain and do some maths. Sorry about that. Ladies and gents, meet the gauge swatch. He's boring. I mean, really boring. Not only do you have to do maths, but you're going to have to knit a square and find a tape measure.

If gauge is important to your knit (such as with patterns like Pooch on Parade Poncho, where you need your knit the right size to fit a certain space) then you are going to have to knit a gauge square. Oh the horror! You can't even get someone else to knit it for you. Agh!

Gauge is the number of stitches and rows you have in a certain area. Almost every pattern you'll bump into will have gauge lurking somewhere near the start. Gauge instructions will look like this: X stitches and Y rows = 10cm (4in)

Measuring gauge

You'll need to knit a square, in the same stitch pattern as the pattern you're about to make, that is a little bigger than 10 by 10cm (4 by 4in). At this point, some people cheat and knit 6 by 6cm (2½ by 2½in). But the rules tell you to do the 10cm (4in) square. Up to you if you want to break them. Just don't come crying to me from the depths of your gargantuan jumper.

1 Cast on the correct number of stitches to make 12cm (4¾in).

2 Knit until the square measures about 12cm (4¾in).

3 Block your square (wet it, pin flat without stretching, let it dry).

4 Measure your stitch count by counting how many stitches there are in 10cm (4in).

5 Measure your row count by counting how many stitches there are in 10cm (4in).

6 Check that your gauge matches up to the gauge of your pattern.

Aaaiiiieeeee! My gauge doesn't match!

Pull yourself together! It can happen to us all. No two knitters knit the same. Not even identical twins. It's been tested. Though not with clones. I'll get back to you on that after more time in the laboratory.

• If your gauge has more stitches than the pattern says, try again using bigger needles.

• If your gauge has fewer stitches than the pattern says, try again with smaller needles.

• If your gauge matches exactly, then you are truly blessed. Hail the yarn gods.

IT'S NOT ALL ABOUT KNITTING

Oi! Where do you think you're going? Now you've learnt to knit your training isn't over. There are some skills that are to knitting what mash and gravy are to meat pies. Alone they're great, but together they're fantabulous. If you keep on learning, you may one day turn yourself into a many-skilled and much-revered Swiss Army Knife of craft. So here are a couple of other useful techniques with which to make your stitching splendiferous. This is going to be the start of a beautiful fibre friendship, I can tell.

Captain Hook

Crochet! The easy-peasy technique of making a crochet chain will save you the fiddlyness of knitting a chain. It's quicker, it's less hassle and you get to wave a hook around.

1 Make a slip knot about 6in (15cm) from the end of the yarn and put it on your hook. Hold your hook in your right hand.

2 Hold the knot between your thumb and middle finger of your left hand.

3 Put the yarn over your index finger of your left hand and hold it against your palm with your last two fingers to keep the yarn taut.

4 Wrap the yarn over the hook from back to front between the hook end and the knot.

5 Pull the yarn through the loop using the hook.

6 Repeat steps 4 and 5 until you chain is the length you want.

Suppliers

These people have been kind enough to send me lovely yarns and shiny craft stuff with which to create this knitty city. If you buy from them give them a woolly wave from *Stitch New York* to return the crafty love.

BUTTONS
All fabulously funky buttons used from Gregory Knopp: www.gregory-knopp.co.uk

YARNS
Knit New Yorkers
Handmade Holly Golightly: Cygnet DK (worsted) yarn in Black and Flesh
Woolly Woody Allen: Cygnet DK (worsted) yarn in Burgundy, Harvest and Flesh
Feisty Fibre Firefighters: Cygnet DK (worsted) yarn in Black, Bright Yellow, Sunshine, Beige and Flesh
Mini Metropolis
Squishy Empire State: Cygnet DK (worsted) yarn in Grey, Twilleys of Stamford Goldfingering in Silver
Small Yellow Taxi: Cygnet DK (worsted) yarn in Sunshine, Black and White
On the Town
Lights, Camera, Action Leg Warmers and Blockbuster Beanie:
When Harry Met Sally: hand-dyed aran (medium-weight) yarn from A Stash Addict dyed in colours inspired by the film poster colours
Muppets Take Manhattan Leg Warmers: Laughing Hens Rooster Almerino Aran in 306 Gooseberry; Texere Yarns Mo Glow Putrid Pink, Vicious Violet, Yucky Yellow and Lurid Lime
Ghostbusters Leg Warmers: Debbie Bliss Cashmerino Aran; Artesano Aran in SFN50 black; Texere Yarns Mo Glow Putrid Pink, Vicious Violet, Yucky Yellow and Lurid Lime
West Side Story Leg Warmers: Laughing Hens Rooster Aran in 310 Rooster Hat; Artesano Aran in 0042 Wester
Pooch on Parade Poncho: Cygnet DK in Red, Royal and White

Home Turf
Big Bad Burger: Sirdar Big Softie in Muffin, Moose, Boho, Chilli, Top Banana
Huge Hot Dog Cushion: Rowan Big Wool in Glamour from Deramores; Sirdar Big Softie in Muffin
Cocktail Teenies: Bramwell Crafts Fine 4ply (sport) in Sunflower (Shimmer, Quacker); Lemon (Sour); Bottle (Pickle); White (Quacker); Scarlet (Sugar)
City Critters
Smash the Angry Ape: Cygnet DK (worsted) in Black
Scram the Alley Cat: Cygnet DK (worsted) in Jaffa
Snap the Sewer Alligator: Cygnet DK (worsted) in Lime, Red and Sunshine
Scuttle the Cockroach: Cygnet DK (worsted) in Chocolate
Guerrilla Gardening
Blooming Bugs: non-biodegradable plastic bags from various shops
Woolly Wildflowers: Cygnet DK (worsted) yarn in Bright Lime, Jaffa, Bright Yellow
Patons Fab DK (worsted) in Bright Pink from Deramores

Websites
Artesano Limited: www.artesanoyarns.co.uk
Bramwell Crafts: www.bramwellcrafts.co.uk
A Stash Addict: www.astashaddict.co.uk and www.etsy.com/shop/AStashAddict
Cygnet Yarns Ltd: www.cygnetyarns.com
Debbie Bliss: www.debbieblissonline.com
Deramores: www.deramores.com
Laughing Hens: www.laughinghens.com
RUCraft: www.rucraft.co.uk
Sirdar: www.sirdar.co.uk
Texere Yarns: www.texere-yarns.co.uk
All other mystery unlabelled stash yarn comes from my huge and mysterious stash. There is much strangeness in there and it appears to multiply while I'm not looking. I hope one day that it will become sentient and aid me in my bid for woolly world domination.

Acknowledgments

Huge woolly hugs to: Katy, my ridiculously patient editor and a fantabulous human being. Camera-wielding genius Jack Kirby for scaling fire escapes, ordering rare steak and lying on ridiculously hot sidewalks on the most awesome three-day book shoot the world has ever known. Mia for her kick-ass design work; Lorna and the Bangwallop folks for the extra pics; Jeni, Anna and everyone at F&W for helping to conjure another city book from the tangle of my words and wild woolly ideas; and my amazing cheerleading agent Carol.

Brigitte, my marvellous mum, a.k.a. night-stitching Madame Molet, Mr Mole, and my ever-impressed brother Max, for putting up with the clouds of yarn from upstairs. The furry feline four for not eating my yarn ends, and my number-one fan Sophie 'Judy' who chose to get married at the same time as my book deadline but made up for it by being disgustingly proud of her sis. Natali, for untangling my snarls, and brand new Betty Bug who inspired bug-flavoured knitting. Ellen for her tireless location wrangling (Go Red Hook!) and Stephen, too. Sarah for stupendous studio support, Emma Toft, my fibre-flinging agony aunt, and Julia Goolia, cheerleader from down under.

Yarn suppliers: Danielle Alinia for bringing the *When Harry Met Sally* yarn to life, Andy from Laughing Hens, Amy from Deramores for hunting down just the right hot dog pink, Joanne from Texere (and for yarn names for Mo Glo), Jane from Sirdar, Katie from Cygnet, and Jenny and Tom from Artesano, and Mary from Bramwell Crafts. Also the film folks on Ravelry forums and Cerridwen on The Hip Forums for her almost endless list of knitting in films, and Wikipedia for helping me work out which ones were set in NYC. The twerrific people of Twitter and Facebook for throwing answers and guffaws my way (you stalkers know how you are, but special thanks to Emsiepopples, Curlyminx, Knitterbird and Ponddrop), Sarah P Corbett for subversive inspiration, Marianne Dimarco-Temkin for encouragement from across the pond, Richard Reynolds: guerrilla gardening guru, and everyone who filled out my NY Brain Picking survey online.

In NYC: Anna 'Mochimochi Land' Hrachovec, Jenna Leigh Teti, and the handsome hound Bandit, who are just brilliant. Jaw-droppingly fabulous Phyllis Howe for helping me find my way about New York's knitty side, and Erin Slonaker for the same. Also the warm woolly welcome from NYC's yarn shops: Purl Soho, La Casita, Knitty City, Lion Brand Studio, Loopy Mango, Downtown Yarns, and Brooklyn General. And Melissa Salzman for distracting me with NYC's finest bloody marys. The splendiferous staff at Tiffany and Co, who put a $36,800 necklace on Handmade Holly and let us shoot in store; the Lyric Diner; and the folks of Red Hook, Brooklyn, for loving our bugs so much we left them there, and Christian Larsen who let us take pictures of a knitted cat on his fire escape, no questions asked.

Robert DeNiro, Woody Allen, Diane Keaton, Al Pacino, and Jerry Seinfeld for keeping me amused while I knit. And, as ever, humongous handmade hugs to my long-suffering Sheepsketcher for rescuing me from yarny riptides, and making me stop knitting and go to sleep before my hands dropped off. This book would be a stitched shambles without you and so would I.

Knitters

Brigitte 'Midnight knitting Madame Molet' Onyskiw, Emma 'Goldenblades91' Pooley, Clare 'Dragonflyclef' Tovey, Tina 'Wickedly Witchy and Lady in Red' Bragaglia, and the fantabulous Katie Lee. Splendiferous stitching friends all. Sorry I made you knit in crazy yarn, ladies. You are all utter stars. All other knits by Lauren 'Deadly Knitshade has lost all feeling in her fingers from knitting a giant burger in a single day' O'Farrell.

About the Author

Author, artist, traveller and giant squid wrestler, Lauren O'Farrell learned to knit while fighting a three-year battle with evil cancer. The combination of chemotherapy, radiotherapy and yarn instilled her with eerie knitting powers while saving her life. She now runs Stitch London, the UK's largest woolly Godzilla of a knitting community (now global, with over 12,500 members in 52 countries worldwide) as Head Woolly Godzilla Wrangler (official title). She is also rumoured to be sneaky stitching graffiti knitter Deadly Knitshade, of Knit the City fame (though she will neither confirm or deny this if you ask).

She lives in London's Crystal Palace (where the concrete dinosaurs roam) with a Sheepsketcher, a flock of knitted pigeons, and Plarchie, an 8m (26ft) giant knitted squid who eats people like the puny human sushi they are. She makes her woolly mischief at the Fleece Station studio in Deptford. It is rumoured she never sleeps. Either that or she has a clone.

Website:
www.whodunnknit.com

Twitter and Instagram:
@deadlyknitshade

Facebook: Whodunnknit

Join Stitch London:
www.stitchLDN.com;
Stalk Knit the City:
www.knitthecity.com

Find out about the Fleece Station:
www.fleecestation.co.uk

DEDICATION

For Max 'Roy' Onyskiw, a brilliant brother and the most hipster dude I will ever know.

For marvellous Mole, ever-encouraging and my unofficial finished item photographer.

And for Julia 'Goolia' Hutabarat, my bestest friend ever and a terrible, but persistent, knitter.

NOTE
Keep all small items used in these projects, such as buttons and beads, out of reach of babies and young children.

A DAVID & CHARLES BOOK
© F&W Media International, LTD 2013

David & Charles is an imprint of F&W Media International, LTD
Brunel House, Forde Close, Newton Abbot, TQ12 4PU, UK

F&W Media International, LTD is a subsidiary of F+W Media Inc.
4700 East Galbraith Road, Cincinnati, OH 45236, USA

First published in the UK and USA in 2013

Text and designs © Lauren O'Farrell 2013
Layout and photography © F&W Media International, LTD 2013

Lauren O'Farrell has asserted her right to be identified as author of this work in accordance with the Copyright, Designs and Patents Act, 1988.

A catalogue record for this book is available from the British Library.

ISBN-13: 978-1-4463-0188-3 paperback
ISBN-10: 1-4463-0188-5 paperback

Printed in China by RR Donnelley
for F&W Media International, LTD
Brunel House, Forde Close, Newton Abbot, TQ12 4PU, UK

10 9 8 7 6 5 4 3 2 1

Publisher Alison Myer
Acquisitions Editor Katy Denny
Editor Jeni Hennah
Project Editor Anna Southgate
Senior Designer and Illustrator Mia Farrant
Photographers Jack Kirby, Mia Farrant and Lorna Yabsley
Production Manager Beverley Richardson

F+W Media Inc. publishes high-quality books on a wide range of subjects. For more great book ideas visit: **www.rucraft.co.uk**